MW01174267

Straight...from hell

The Journey from Bondage to Freedom

By Donna L. Frank

First published by Dog Ear Publishing
4010 W. 86th Street, Ste H
Indianapolis, IN 46268
www.dogearpublishing.net

ISBN: 978-159858-344-1

This book is printed on acid-free paper.

Printed in the United States of America

Dedication

This book is dedicated to those who are stumbling through life in a state of brokenness and confusion but continued to fall forward. It is dedicated to people who feel they have been forever lost and to those who have simply lost their way. Your resiliency, your courage, your willingness to continue to push that elephant up the stairs is proof that you will make it. We have been pressed but not crushed, persecuted but not abandoned. God alone is enough: for all of us. This book is dedicated to everyone who refuses to give up. Continue to stand. God will meet you there.

Acknowledgements

There are a number of people I would like to thank, without whom this story would never have been told. Primarily I thank God; it is only through His divine protection, guidance and provision that this book is possible.

I would like to thank my Mom and my sister, both of whom have not only lived this nightmare with me, but have continued to walk with me into freedom. My friends have been invaluable in seeing me through this process: Emily, Paul & Charity, Kim & Adam, Mr. Philip & Miss Carol. Thank you for your prayers and your patience.

To Pastors Dino & DeLynn Rizzo and everyone at Healing Place Church, thank you for truly being a healing place for a hurting world. I would like to thank Dave and Joyce Meyer for the sacrifices they make daily to bring truth to the world and hope to the hopeless. To my prayer partners and supporters, thank you for your continued belief in this work.

And finally to Pastor Alliece, who not only recognized that I was in a ditch but was willing to get into the ditch with me until I was well enough to get out. Thank you for never giving up on me, even when I gave up on myself. Thank you for laying down your life for me, and for so many others like me. One day, when I grow up, I hope to be like you.

Therefore we also, since we are surrounded by so great a cloud of witnesses, let us lay aside every weight, and the sin which so easily ensnares us, and let us run with endurance the race that is set before us, looking unto Jesus, the author and finisher of our faith, who for the joy that was set before Him endured the cross, despising the shame, and has sat down at the right hand of the throne of God. For consider Him who endured such hostility from sinners against Himself, lest you become weary and discouraged in your souls.

Hebrews 12:1–3

All glory, all honor and all praise to God!

Chapter One

"In the beginning God created the heavens and the earth. Now the earth was formless and empty, darkness was over the surface of the deep..."

Genesis 1:1–2

I sometimes tell people that I was raised by orangutans. My parents did their very best, but they simply didn't have the tools they needed to raise healthy children. The suffocating pain and lack in their own lives affected many of the decisions they made in raising their kids. I love them and I thank God for them. I am who I am today because of them. I do not believe that anyone enters parenthood with the hope or expectation that they will completely destroy their child's sense of self. If you feel that your parents failed you, I suggest that you make a choice to forgive them and move on. Make a decision to release them from your heart so that all of you can be free. My hope is that this book will give you some tools to do just that.

My childhood was less than I would have liked it to be. I felt as though I was continually reaching for something that I couldn't have. I longed to be loved and instead I was abused. I longed for acceptance and instead I was abandoned. I longed for affirmation and instead I found shame. Those became the foundation of my life: abuse, abandonment and shame. From that shaky beginning I entered into a painful existence that would cycle upon itself for the next thirty years. This is my story.

At the same time that my dad was being stitched up from an alcohol-related car wreck, I was born at a military hospital in Rhode Island. My mother was scared and alone, and hoping desperately that my arrival would force Dad to sober up. My mom didn't drink and she worked a lot. With two kids under the age of two and an alcoholic husband she didn't have time for much else. She was a nurse and worked very hard at being a good one. I realize now that her occupation was one of the few things she felt she had any control over. My dad was in the Marine Corps and was a very good soldier. He was so good, in fact, that he could regain rank almost as quickly as he lost it. Booze, violence and women; all of them downfalls. I had no idea that I was next in line for those same generational curses.

My parents met when Mom moved from Canada to the southern U.S. after graduating from nursing school. She and some of her classmates decided that they wanted to experience life a little before returning to the small farming towns in which they grew up. Mom would eventually meet a charming, handsome Marine who talked her into bed. Before long she found herself pregnant. They were married immediately and a short time later she miscarried. She didn't go to the hospital. Her premarital pregnancy would become part of her shame and one of her long-held secrets.

Over the next few years Dad's drinking, violent temper and extramarital exploits continued. As so many women mistakenly assume, Mom thought that having children would improve the marriage. The arrival of my sister did nothing to tame my father, nor did my arrival sixteen months later. With the Vietnam War in full swing, Dad opted out of the military when his service was up.

My family was typical of societal dysfunction: my father was ex-military with a severe drinking problem and uncontrolled rage; my mother was a workaholic with a high level of codependency. We never had a lot of money, and often we didn't have enough. Living in lack can create shame, but in my case it only added to what was already there.

My childhood was rife with abuse. I was sexually abused by my father and grandfather from infancy, and I was politely abused by a next-door neighbor. I say politely because the neighbor never physically hurt me, as all I had to do was sit on his lap and let him touch me. Sometimes he gave me candy and sometimes he gave me money. I was too young to recognize that for what it was, and by the time I did, I believed that it too was my fault.

People have asked me why I never told anyone about the abuse. That strikes me as an odd question, as I wonder why nobody ever told me that it was abuse. I don't remember when it started; it just always was. If something happens to a child at home, at Grandma's house and every time you go outside, it feels pretty normal. It doesn't feel good, but it feels normal. And, if your dad is telling you that it's just part of growing up and that everyone does it, why would you question that? After all, he's Dad. He must know.

Children who are raised in abuse have an amazing capacity for altering their reality into something they can handle. I lived in constant fear of people finding out how wretched I truly was. I knew that I was dirty, all the way through my heart, and I knew that the fear that I walked in would eventually cripple me. But, I also knew that one day Dad was really going to show up and take me fishing. I knew that one day Mom and Dad would really be happy. I knew that one day my sister would laugh, or at least smile. I had to believe these things for my own fragile sanity. I had to believe, even when all evidence pointed to the contrary.

Within a couple of years of moving to Canada, Mom and Dad bought a house and settled into the chaotic rhythm of abuse, deception and fear. The early years of my childhood are little more than a blur. I remember horses. My sister and I both rode in western shows at local events. I remember Black

Jet, the foal that Dad promised to give me. I was so excited when he was finally born. He was pure black except for a white marking on his forehead that looked, to me, like a star. I fed him with a baby bottle because he was sick. I watched the vet give him giant needles. I watched him die when the needles didn't work. Black Jet was gone. Shortly thereafter my dad sold the other horses. We put the trophies and ribbons away and moved on. I don't ever remember grieving over Black Jet, or anything else. We just moved on.

Small towns are funny; everyone knows each other's business but they act like they don't. Even as a child I knew whose dad was having an affair with the bank teller and which of the trucker's wives had 'company' over when the big rigs were gone. Looking back, I think that most of the people in our town were afraid of my father. I have to assume that's the reason that no one ever tried to intervene. It was not unusual for the police to be at our house; furniture smashed and Mom crying. I would sometimes watch the neighbors watching us. They would peek through their curtains or curiously, decide it was time to walk that dog that hadn't been walked since the last time the police were there. They watched, but they never helped. I remember standing at our living room window watching my mother run down the street, Dad chasing her and threatening to beat her to death. I know I was not the only one standing at a window and watching. Dad didn't catch her that day. Instead he fell on the ice and sprained his ankle. She did get beat, but not that day and not to death. And, they continued to watch.

I hated the neighbors for not helping us and I hated our teachers for not getting involved. I understand now that they were probably afraid for their own safety, as Dad was extremely dangerous and nowhere near stable. But I somehow felt that we should have mattered enough, to somebody, for them to take a risk. We didn't. They continued to watch and we continued to die.

I never got a medical diagnosis as a child, but I was a mess. I can remember standing in the yard beside our house, looking into the sky and wondering when the aliens would come back for me. I just knew I wasn't of this world; I couldn't be. If I were of this world, I would understand things and not be so afraid. I would be like other kids and not feel so bad all the time. I would know how to live, instead of only wanting to die. I was so full of fear that sometimes it was hard to even breathe.

As a child I developed a system, of sorts, to help me through. I took a shower most mornings before school. If I dropped the soap once then it meant something bad was going to happen that day. If I dropped it twice then something horrible was going to happen. If I dropped it a third time then it meant it was too dangerous to leave the house. I would finish my shower, go downstairs and drink a big glass of whatever we had in the fridge. I would then spin around in circles until I threw up. Usually, once I threw up I was considered sick enough to stay home. It was a good plan for a while. I also had a yellow blanket, which was more white than yellow and more of a towel than a blanket. I slept with it every night and played with it every day. I talked to it, cried into it and covered my head with it when the shouting got too loud. I also had two pink blankets, which really were pink and really were blankets. They were on my bed, and they were very worn. They were so worn that instead of being smooth they were covered with those little balls of fluff that nowadays get shaved off with those tiny clippers. Pink Blanket (only the light pink one was named) made me feel safe. So, when the fear got so out of control that I thought I would die, I picked off the little pink balls and ate them. I reasoned that if it made me feel safe on the outside, then, if it were inside me, I would feel safe there too. It didn't work, but I kept trying. In the absence of true solutions, almost anything is better than nothing.

I used to walk to school every day with my best friend from next door. (This was prior to my 'soap and blanket theory' days so I was completely adrift). We had gotten halfway to school when I told her that I had forgotten something. I told her to go ahead to class and that I would meet her there. There is a half-mile racetrack in my hometown, beside which is a set of covered bleachers. It was the middle of a long Canadian winter and the snow was up to my thighs. I remember sitting down on the bleachers and crying. I had crawled under the bleachers, over the empty beer bottles and trash, and found a piece of broken glass. I had taken off my mittens and pulled up the sleeve of my coat as far as I could. I was tracing the veins on my wrist with the glass; not pushing hard enough to cut, and not exactly sure how to do it. I thought of God and hoped He wouldn't be too mad. I didn't know a lot about Him, but I was pretty sure He was supposed to be in charge of the world. The wind was fierce and cutting, swirling snow into heavy drifts. I sat and watched the wind, staring across our frozen town. I tried to think of a reason not to do it, but pain and emptiness blew through me. About the time I had gathered up the courage to push the glass into my skin, I thought of Mom. I thought of how she would feel when she found me, and how sad she would be. My mom was sad a lot. When Dad wasn't beating her up or stealing her car he was running around with other women or lighting the house on fire. Mom had a lot to be sad about. That was the only thought that stopped me from opening my vein and slowly bleeding to death in my snowsuit; I didn't want my mom to be sad. Codependency had taken hold of me before I was in third grade.

I wiped my face, pulled down my sleeve and got my mittens back on. I decided to tell Mom goodbye before I left so she wouldn't be sad. I started the trudge home, tears freezing to my cheeks. She was standing on the picnic table hanging clothes on the line as I struggled through the back yard. We didn't have a dryer, so year-round our laundry blew outside in the wind. She saw me through the snow and called to me.

"Donna, what are you doing here? You're supposed to be in school." Her mouth was full of clothespins.

"I need to talk to you Mom." I was now within fifteen feet of her.

"You need to go to school. You're already late. Go on now, we'll talk tomorrow before school." Mom was working the evening shift so I wouldn't see her again that day. "Donna, whatever it is can wait. Do you have homework you didn't do? Is that why you don't want to go to school?" She was still hanging up clothes, blowing on her hands to keep them from freezing in the sub-zero weather.

"Mom, I need to talk to you." I was now about ten feet away, my face red from crying. She snapped out a towel to hang it on the line.

"What, Donna? What?"

I looked at my boots, buried far beneath the snow and said, "Mom, I don't want to be alive anymore."

I spent much of that morning sitting on her lap. She was baffled, afraid and too wrapped up in her own confusion and pain to understand mine. She tried to find out what was going on, but there was much I didn't tell her. The vacuum of pain I lived in was too vast for me to even think about, never mind articulate. Dad had already told me that she knew about him touching me, and how painful it would be if we talked about it. I was never certain if the 'painful' part meant that he would beat me or her, or if it would just hurt her heart. Either way, I did not want to be responsible for any more pain. At the time I didn't know that he was lying.

I was seven or eight years old when I made that first suicide attempt. That started my long journey through therapists, psych appointments, and medication. All attempts ended in futility, and some made me sicker than I already was. I am not, by any means, condemning medication or mental health professionals. I'm just saying that it didn't work for me.

Mom didn't know, until years later, about the abuse. When she found out she took us away in the middle of the night and put us in hiding. We stayed with relatives until she was able to get a restraining order and file for divorce. She had to stay with other relatives, as there was a good possibility that if Dad found her he would kill her. She reasoned that even if he killed her, at least we would be okay. We all survived that ordeal and no one died, at least not physically.

In my brokenness and codependency, I thought that I had caused the divorce and made Dad leave us. I missed him being there, in spite of the abuse. The deception that abuse creates imbedded confusion in many areas of my life, some of which I'm still sorting out today. As a child it's difficult to separate sex and affection, particularly if you've only ever known abuse. That separation did not become any clearer for me as an adult. It has only been through my relationship with God that I have learned that love, sex and pain are not supposed to be a package deal.

I cried a whole lot as a kid. If anyone looked at me for too long I would burst into tears. I was consumed by fear and afraid of everything and everybody. I was ruled by the what-ifs and the possibilities of what dreadful thing might happen next. Fear completely ruled me until the age of eleven. Then I discovered anger. It happened one day in a locker room at our local ice rink. The coach had yelled at me in front of the team. Everyone, myself included, expected me to cry. Instead of tears welling up, this volcano of anger rose from within me. I didn't cry. I simply took off my jersey, threw it across the room and told him what he could do with it. I picked up my gear and walked out. I didn't cry again for a very long time.

I made an important decision that day in the locker room. For years I had witnessed my mom getting beat and my sister and I being abused. I recognized, that day, that there was always going to be a winner and a loser. From what I had seen, men won and women lost. Something shifted in my spirit, and I determined that I would not continue to lose.

Anger, like all the other addictions that would follow, became a short-term friend and a long-term enemy. It became my protection, my companion and my hope. It eventually became my lover, my motivation, and my identity. For the first time in my life I was on the winning side of fear, and I loved it. Anger, coupled with my constant thoughts of suicide, was a near-fatal combination. I was explosive, unpredictable, and I didn't care if I lived or died.

Everything that anger promised me; power, control, and courage, was eventually stripped from me. But that story will come later.

My sister Brenda is sixteen months older than me and acted as my self-appointed guardian. She was the one who would be pulled from class to go and find me when I ran away from school. She was the one that, when the fighting at home got completely out of control, would take me by the hand and lead me to the other room. She was the one who would dry my tears and tell me that it would be all right, even though we both knew that it wouldn't be. I believed her as often as I could. Looking back, that's a lot of pressure to put on a ten-year-old.

One time, before the divorce, we were in the kitchen when Dad attacked Mom. His voice had gone from anger to mania and there was nothing behind his eyes. The table had already been swept clean and thrown over. He was dangerously close to the knife drawer. Brenda took me by the hand and led me into the living room. We sat side by side on the couch, holding hands and not speaking. I was crying but she wasn't. She almost never cried. Our couch was against the wall that separated the living room from the kitchen. I was sitting as close to her as I could, waiting for the screaming to stop. Dad's fist came through the wall between us, missing both of us by inches. Brenda stood up, pulled me off the couch and led me outside. We stayed in the yard beside the house until we heard the car squeal out of the driveway. We went back inside, got Mom a cold cloth and started cleaning up the kitchen.

That is a snapshot of our childhood.

Chapter Two

"...But when you are tempted, he will also provide a
way out so that you can stand up under it."

1 Corinthians 10:13

I was probably ten years old the first time I got high. One of my younger cousins had marijuana plants that were ready to be harvested. My grandfather had been growing pot for years, having his son sell it to kids at his school. It didn't seem unusual to me that my nine-year-old cousin had access to plants, heat lamps and rolling papers. That was life; you did what you had to do to survive.

Thirty years ago, typical pre-teens were not involved in drugs. But we were not typical kids and we certainly didn't come from a typical family. Sexual abuse, of which most of my paternal cousins were victims, forces you to grow up quickly in a lot of areas. Sadly, it completely paralyzes you in other areas.

My cousins and I were staying at my aunt's house while all of the adults went down to the bar for a few drinks. Brenda was in charge because she was the oldest. She was probably eleven or so. She had been in charge for a couple of years so she knew how it worked. One of our parents would call home every couple of hours to make sure everything was okay; meaning that no one was bleeding, the house wasn't on fire and Mike wasn't having a seizure. Several hours into the evening one parent would sneak home to spy on us, but that was usually Aunt Anna who was always too drunk to spy effectively. While waiting for the first phone call, we developed a plan. Immediately after the call, we put on our coats and ran the half-mile or so through the bush to where the plants were. We filled our pockets with as many leaves as we could and ran back to the house in time for the next phone call. Mike pulled out his lamps and set up shop on the kitchen table. We had already dealt out a card game that we could pick up at the first sign of trouble. One of the younger cousins was posted at the window to watch for headlights. As soon as the headlights were spotted everything was hidden and the cards were picked up. We heard Aunt Anna fall down the hill and into the side of the house before she peered in at us through the window. We pretended not to see her until she busted through the back door, telling us how boring we were to watch. We shrugged, played our fake card game and waited for her to leave. Once she headed back to the bar we finished drying the plants, went outside and got high.

That night I found a new way to cope. It wasn't so much the high as the release. For the first time in my life, I had stepped above the pain. It didn't go away, but it at least backed up. It gave me hope that it was possible to separate myself from the pain. Up until that day, we had been one.

I was standing in the schoolyard the following Monday, not really believing that I had smoked marijuana. I told myself that it didn't matter and that I wouldn't do it again. I told myself that I had only done it because everyone else did. Standing there I knew, the next time drugs were offered I would grab hold and never let go.

The town I grew up in had a population of about three hundred. We had a primary school, two gas stations, two general stores and a bank. We had one hotel and five churches. I went to church as a child, but I don't remember ever hearing the Gospel. I knew God, and it seemed obvious to me (looking at my life) that He was mad at me for something. I had heard about Jesus, but didn't understand that He was alive and could have an impact on my life. I would try to memorize the Bible verses on Sunday morning as I walked to church. The verses meant nothing to me other than the gold star we got if we knew it. I was starving for gold stars. I went because I was supposed to go, and because I always kept a nickel of the fifteen cents I was supposed to put in the offering plate. I was about twelve when I decided that if Mom wasn't going to church, neither was I. From then on we all stayed home, and whatever miniscule tie to rightness that had been in my life was now gone.

After Dad had left, I answered to no one. Mom had been either afraid of me or afraid for me since my suicide attempt. She still worked rotating shifts so my sister and I were home alone a lot of the time. We did have a curfew, but there was no one around to enforce it. We did whatever we wanted, whenever we wanted, with whomever we wanted.

The friends we had were just like us. Nobody had any money to speak of. All of our families were ripe with abuse, alcoholism and dysfunction. It wasn't unusual for anyone in our crowd to have bruises or lacerations from a family disagreement, but it was never mentioned. We were all the same; just trying to stay alive long enough to get out.

I had started playing sports when I was young and that helped a lot with the loneliness and rejection. I discovered early that scoring a goal made people cheer, not just for the goal, but for me. I was still starving for gold stars. I was pretty good at most of the sports I played because I practiced all the time. Often I didn't have anyone to play with (that happens when your dad is a violent alcoholic and the whole towns knows it) so I would spend hours throwing the ball at my bounce-back net or shooting a puck against my basement wall. I played hockey on the river everyday from the time it froze until the day it thawed. I eventually played on an all-star hockey team in our area. Although the crowd cheered and people slapped my back, I was continually scanning the crowd to see if Mom had come to watch. She almost never did, not because she didn't want to, but because she was busy. I could never score enough goals to dull the ache.

I was about twelve years old the first time somebody called me 'butch'. I was walking across the parking lot of our arena, heading home after a game. I didn't know what it meant, but I knew it wasn't nice. It may have been because I had short hair and wore jeans all the time, or they may have recognized the spirit in me before I did. Either way, the word felt more like a title than an insult and, even without definition, it became part of me.

I wasn't good at being a girl. I was stocky, athletic and I could figure out how to fix things. I didn't want Barbie dolls and EZ Bake Ovens. I wanted GI Joe and Tonka trucks. My sister was pretty, smart and popular. I was the dumpy kid with a lisp that cried a lot. Then I was the angry kid with a lisp that fought a lot. Life was decidedly bad.

Brenda, my sister, was good at being a girl. She got good grades, was invited to parties and had more boyfriends than she wanted. I was only one grade behind her in school, so our teachers often remarked on the contrast between us. I never felt that I measured up, so I quit trying altogether.

We both belonged to Brownies and then Girl Guides. Every year we had to put on a skit at the regional rally. One year we were told that we would be performing "The Wizard of Oz". It was very exciting, waiting to see who would be chosen for the lead roles. I knew that Brenda would be Dorothy, with the little dog and solos. I was hoping to be the Tin Man, but I expected I would probably be the Cowardly Lion. As it turned out, I was neither. I was cast as a yellow brick. While Brenda danced around singing songs, I laid on the floor wearing a cardboard box and yellow tights. She stepped on me every time she danced past. Small wonder that we beat each other senseless when no one was around.

I don't remember where we got it from, but in our early teens we started playing with a Ouija board. We read horoscopes, attempted spells and tried to call on spirits. The whole group of us would go to the graveyard late at night and attempt séances and practice levitation in our living room. To my knowledge, none of us had any type of training in any of this. If there was organized witchcraft in our area, I didn't know about it. If I had, I have no doubt that I would have willingly joined. I desperately needed power in my life, and at that time I didn't care where it came from.

My first day of high school was pivotal for me. I got off the bus, scared and lost, having no idea how to cope with myself or any of these people. I had just walked through the door when a girl grabbed me and threw me against a locker. Without thinking, I grabbed her by the throat and threw her into a wall. I stood there with my hand tight around her neck, wondering what to do. I looked at her face and saw fear; hers, not mine. What a rush! For the first time I could remember, violence was a good thing. She told me through her tears that she was sorry, that she thought I was somebody else. I told her very calmly that she should be careful, as she may end up getting hurt. I let go of her throat and she slid down the wall. By the time I picked up my books and found my classroom, rumors were rampant. As it turned out, this girl was the school bully. Apparently she and I had been dating the same guy over the summer, and she was mad. I had no particular feelings about this guy so it meant nothing to me, but that little skirmish in the hall bought me some newfound respect. Kids would give me cigarettes, money and drugs, to protect them from her. I often wondered who would protect me, from me.

I got through high school because of soccer. I played all sports as though it were life and death. I was fairly talented and had no fear of injury or expulsion. When I wasn't playing soccer I was getting high or copying my sister's homework. I tried to take all the same classes that she had taken the year before. I would re-write her essays when I had time, but often I would just white-out her name and hand it in. She was still looking after me and there was still nobody watching.

I started playing women's softball when I was about thirteen. This was my first up-close exposure to lesbians. My teammates would talk about 'that team' and the type of women who played for them. I was terrified and fascinated. They were bold and obnoxious and didn't care what we thought of them. By the time I was seventeen I had bought a car and started playing for 'that team'. Within three months I was going to gay bars every weekend and had been involved with two of the players on the team.

The day that I signed up with them I had a new team and a new family. For the first time in my life I felt accepted. I didn't know if it was wrong and I didn't care. I had been searching for that feeling forever.

My drug use and new friends were interfering with my schoolwork so I quit. Mom told me I couldn't use drugs in her house so I moved out. I moved in with a woman from the team that was a dozen years older than me. Our only common ground was drugs, baseball and bars. I immediately forgot about all my old friends. I lived for Friday nights at the club and was fully immersed in the culture. I learned the language, the symbols and the rules. I read 'Stone Butch Blues' and felt I was complete.

I lived with that woman until she made a bet with me that I couldn't convert a straight co-worker. I won the bet and moved in with my next ex.

Within two weeks of meeting Jen I knew she was an alcoholic. That didn't really matter to me, as people had been telling me that I was an alcoholic since I was fourteen. She was very cute and very curious about the life that I led. I was more than happy to introduce her to another world. She had a four-year-old daughter and a violent ex-husband. They weren't divorced yet, and didn't have a real good grasp on the whole idea of separation. Floyd was in and out of her life for the duration of our 5-year relationship.

Jen knew from our first date that we shouldn't be together. She tried to break up with me but my pride and fear of being alone wouldn't allow it. We drank, did drugs, fought and made up. Neither of us had any idea how to function in society. The highs were incredibly high and the lows were without measure. Suicide was a near continual thought. I imagined driving into a rock cut at high speed, being stabbed by one of Jen's lovers, being shot down by police in a drug bust, or getting so high that my brain just exploded. None of it happened, but it wasn't for lack of trying.

I never hit Jen, having sworn never to be like Dad. (I somehow missed the fact that I was already an abusive alcoholic who spent her money and ran around all the time.) Nevertheless, violence circled around us continually. It seemed I was always in the middle of a bar brawl or fighting with one of her lovers. Sometimes the police came and sometimes they didn't. I seldom went to the hospital unless the police forced me to go. The last time I went I had cracked ribs, a broken nose and the medical staff had concerns about internal bleeding. My jaw was swollen on one side and I couldn't open my mouth wide enough to smoke. The doctor told me that if I had taken that punch a quarter of an inch higher, my jawbone would have shattered and been driven into my brain. He looked at me and told me I was a quarter of an inch away from being dead. My only thought was 'so close, and yet so far'. I left the hospital and returned to my life of insanity.

Through what I now know to be God's grace I managed to stay alive and out of prison, narrowly on both counts. I've had a guy throw a knife at my head from across the table, received multiple death threats and been in more car accidents than I care to count. I've been involved in illegal activities of various forms and should probably still be doing time somewhere. God's hand was definitely upon me.

Chapter Three

"...and the Spirit of God was hovering
over the face of the waters."

Genesis 1:2

By the time I was twenty I was in the detox unit of a psychiatric hospital and unable to function in society. The year prior I'd had eleven jobs and had moved a half-dozen times. I was a mass of untreated pain, oozing with hatred, contempt and self-loathing. I had no idea where to turn or how to escape the torment.

About a week after I got to detox they gave me a three-hour pass and a city bus ticket. I was supposed to go across town and meet with an addictions counselor for some type of assessment. As I was riding the bus I was racking my brain as to where I could get a thousand dollars to buy an ounce of cocaine. I couldn't go back home, since part of the reason I went to detox was because I owed some people money and had to get off the street for a while. There was nobody left in my life that trusted me enough to loan it to me, as it was certain that I would never pay it back. I couldn't even think of anyone I could steal it from. My house of cards was rapidly tumbling down.

I got off the bus a couple of blocks from my destination and walked into a McDonald's. I ordered a value meal and continued to scheme. At the time, McDonald's had some type of promotion related to Scrabble. With every food purchase you got game pieces with letters on them, which you were supposed to collect to win prizes. I opened my game pieces as I ate my French fries and laid the letters out in front of me; D,E,A, and D. I looked around the restaurant and then towards the ceiling. It was the first time in a very long while that I had thought about God.

As with all good codependent excitement-junkies, I met a woman in detox who seemed to be the perfect match. She was a heterosexual heroine addict with morals as questionable as mine. She was moved from detox to a treatment across town, so a few days later I requested to be sent to the same center. Within twenty-four hours we had left the treatment center and moved into the basement of a drug dealer whose wife we had met in detox. We got high within moments of walking through the door. I left a few days later, having no regard for my life or hers.

As I was leaving that first treatment center the counselor said, "Donna, you're going to leave, you're going to use and you're going to die." I looked him in the eye and said, "I'm okay with that." I had no fear of dying, being unable to imagine an existence worse than my current life. My real fear was that I would continue to live.

I moved back in with Jen, on the condition that the guy she was living with move out. I know that sounds crazy but sanity is sometimes circumstance-dependent. He moved out, I moved in and the cycle continued. I tried hard to stay sober through will power and a 12-step program. I failed consistently for several months. I thought that getting clean might alleviate the pain. I was unwilling to change the people, places and things in my life so I continued to stumble. Although I never used cocaine again after that scare in McDonald's, I continued to drink and smoke dope. I didn't really believe that people got sober and stayed sober. I couldn't imagine wanting that.

I came home one afternoon with a balloon for Jen. It had a picture of a duck wearing rubber boots and holding an umbrella. It said something about being under the weather. Jen had been sick for several days, not being able to keep food down. Neither of us were drinking heavily at that time, so the illness was unexplained. I walked in, kissed her on the cheek and handed her the balloon. She smiled, lit a cigarette and handed it to me. She motioned to the couch as she lit a cigarette for herself. I sat down on the couch, across from the chair she was in. I asked her how she was feeling.

"I need to talk to you, Jake". (Jake was a street name I had picked up several years earlier. Most of the people I knew called me that, some of whom still don't know my real name). She took a deep breath and continued, "I went to the doctors today".

"What did he say? Is everything okay?" I started to move towards her but she shook her head. I sat back down on the couch. "What did he say?"

She took a drag of her cigarette and looked me in the eyes. "I'm pregnant, Jake".

Cancer would have been less of a surprise. She looked away from me and took another drag. I got up and touched the balloon with my cigarette. The loud pop made her jump. I walked out of the apartment in shock.

I wish I could tell you that I left that relationship. I didn't. I was so confused and hurt and angry that I could barely breathe. I thought the pain would kill me. I returned to the apartment later that night. It was suffocatingly quiet. Neither of us knew what to say to each other for days.

Within a couple of months I was offered a bed at another treatment center. This time it was a 28-day residential program for women, located in Toronto. I had never been to a big city before. I was terrified to go and terrified to stay. Jen took me to the bus station and we had another huge fight as the bus pulled up. I boarded the bus hoping it would crash.

I had to change buses in Kingston, the city where my sister then lived. I called her from the station and asked her to come and pick me up. We were accustomed to getting crazy calls from each other, asking for help to clean up whatever mess we were currently in. She told me she would come, but then asked why I was at the bus station. I said I was on my way to treatment, but that I had changed my mind. She paused, and then suggested that maybe treatment was a good idea. I knew she had been concerned about my drug use for several years. She was, in fact, the only person in my life that I ever recall questioning me about how much I used. She told me that she had to go to work and couldn't come to pick me up. She told me to get on the bus and go to treatment. I couldn't believe she wouldn't help me.

I somehow managed to get to Toronto, navigate the subway system, and talk to the only friendly bus driver in the city. He got me to my stop and pointed me in the direction of the treatment center. It was located on the grounds of an old psychiatric hospital. I drug my suitcase across the yard thinking 'here I go again'.

A tiny woman with a very kind face met me at the door and took me into the office. She told me she was going to fill out my intake papers so she had to ask me a few questions. We got through the name, rank and serial number business pretty quickly. Then she wanted to know about my drug use.

"Okay Donna, it says on your application that you are a drug addict. What is your drug of choice?"

"Cocaine", I answered.

"Do you have any other addictions, dear?" she asked with a smile.

"No." I was a firm believer in one-word answers.

"How often did you use cocaine, dear?" I shrugged so she continued. "Did you use it everyday?" she persisted.

"Probably" I said.

"Do you drink?"

"Some," I said, "but only when I use." I was tired and scared.

"Donna," she said gently, "you told me that you use drugs everyday. Does that mean that you drink everyday as well?" This interview was not going well.

By the end of the application we had determined that I was addicted to cocaine, alcohol, marijuana and prescription medication. I had left out the speed, LSD, and various other drugs that I used on what I considered to be a recreational basis. On paper, I really looked like a wreck.

Treatment was different this time. For the first time in my life I had people telling me that they thought I could make it. I heard words like dysfunctional and codependent. Until then, I had no idea that not everybody lived like I did. I thought that everybody ate goulash for Thanksgiving after their dad had kicked the turkey across the room in a drunken brawl. I thought that every family had lost an uncle to an execution-style murder. I thought that everybody was secretly abusing their kids. I was shocked to learn that my family was not normal.

I started to learn about a Higher Power, some type of god that loved me and could still the screaming madness within me. They told me that this god wanted to help me. I didn't know much about anything, but I was sick enough and hurt enough to give it a try.

I met some good people there. I learned about discipline and accountability, and that I didn't have to be controlled by my emotions. What a concept! I started to believe that I might actually be able to survive without a continual supply of narcotics and alcohol flowing through me. I wasn't certain that I could pull it off, but I was willing to give it a try. For the first time in my life, I had hope.

Hope is a delicate thing. I believe it has to be handled with care, particularly when children are involved. My sister and I grew up with an absence of hope. For years we had a poster on our bedroom wall that said, 'It's always darkest before it's pitch black'. I remember Mom telling us repeatedly, "Expect nothing, girls. You'll never be disappointed." The only thing worse than falling short of your expectations is never having any in the first place. It's no wonder that by the time I was twelve I was certain that the light at the end of the tunnel was an oncoming train.

I would like to tell you that I walked out of that treatment center and lived happily ever after. That didn't happen. I had stopped pumping drugs into my system, but I was still fanatically codependent and terrified of being alone. Almost immediately I re-entered the same relationship that I had so desperately tried to escape. I moved back in with Jen, who was now several months pregnant. The complete absence of self-esteem in my life allowed me to stay. I stayed as other lovers came and went; I stayed as she continued to drink and use; I stayed because I didn't know that I deserved any different. My reasoning was 'better the devil you know than the devil you don't'. I didn't realize that some people had relationships without any devils.

Haley was born in the middle of January during a blizzard. She was four minutes old the first time I held her. I immediately fell in love with her. Jen's oldest daughter, Felicia, had just turned seven. I had taught her to tie her shoes, ride a bike and throw a ball. Floyd had joined the navy and now lived on the other side of the country. He saw the girls, and Jen, whenever he was home on leave. Jen continued being Jen, but I no longer knew how to be Jake. Without the drugs to dull the pain, it finally became too much to bear. Haley was three-and-a-half when I left.

I moved into a one-bedroom apartment on the ground floor with a window that looked out into the parking lot. It was filthy, it smelled bad and there were some kind of silver bugs that crawled up the drain if I forgot to put the plug in. Jen and I never fought about me leaving. We both knew it was five years overdue. Haley and Felicia didn't understand why I left and continually asked me when I was coming home. My heart broke every time.

I kept going to 12-step meetings and I stayed sober. I can't say that I had any real victory in my life, but I wasn't drinking or using drugs. I still had anger problems, a bad attitude and a myriad of other issues. Within weeks of moving into my apartment, I had met my next ex. I had intended it to be a short-term thing, but my raging codependency wouldn't allow it. Beth and I started dating and the day I finished school I moved to Toronto to live with her. She too was an active member in a 12-step program and had the same amount of clean time that I did (almost four years). She was very different than Jen, but I soon discovered that I was still attracted to really broken people.

We started going to a gay-positive church where we received instruction about the "misinterpretation" of the Bible regarding gays. I was erroneously taught that King James was a pedophile and raging homophobic whom had the scriptures altered to condemn homosexuality instead of pedophilia. I was taught that God created all of us in His image and therefore, since 'He made me gay' it would be an insult to Him not to live my life with pride. The church made it possible to love God and continue to live in sin. Since I didn't know anything about the Bible I took the minister at his word. I've since learned that this is a dangerous practice in any situation.

Beth and I were eventually married at that church. We stood before God and professed our love and commitment to one another. I truly believed that would make God, and me, happy. I had no idea how completely deceived I was.

As anyone who has lived the lifestyle knows, life as a homosexual is very myopic. I lived in a gay neighborhood, attended gay meetings, played on gay sports teams and worked in gay-positive environments. It was easy to believe that my lifestyle was acceptable because anyone who had different views was immediately cut out of my life. My partner and I seemed to have a great relationship; we had good jobs, drove nice cars and lived in nice places. Without the intervention of God I would have had a very acceptable life, at least until I died.

What people couldn't see from the outside was the unsettledness and torment that continually plagued me. Shortly after our wedding I had my first round of debilitating depression. At the time I was a welfare field worker for Social

Services. I had a caseload of about four hundred people, all of whom lived in an area of Toronto commonly referred to as the 'gay ghetto'. HIV and AIDS were rampant and drug cocktails had not yet been perfected. Most of my clients were in various stages of dying. Every week I watched twenty and thirty year-olds die. They came to me when they needed diapers and liquid food, and then their lovers and families came to me to set up death benefits. After two years the depression was so bad that I couldn't leave the house. I started therapy again and went on medication. I believed that my depression was work-related. I never went back to that job, going back to school instead.

My partner had battled depression for years and often suffered with poor health. We got married in March, and by November of that year she was off work on disability. She did not work again during our ten-year relationship.

Due to Beth's illness we eventually moved from the city, back to the small town I grew up in. The local lesbians were as friendly and accommodating as when I left. I unpacked my sports gear and signed with 'that team' again. Within six months I had started work at the factory and bought a house. The outside once again looked good but the emptiness inside me continued like a sucking chest wound.

By this time I was ten years sober. I was still controlled by lust, gambling, and fits of rage. I consistently made bad financial decisions and was almost completely consumed by the flesh. I wasn't drinking or using drugs, but I had found new avenues for my addictions. I continued to go to meetings and was told to put first things first. As long as I didn't pick up a drink, I was permitted to keep all my other insanity.

I had another bout of depression, this one worse than the last. I was unable to go to work, leave the house or even take a shower without having someone in the room with me. I was incapacitated by fear. I didn't talk to anyone and needed direction as to when to sleep, eat and brush my teeth. My life felt completely empty and I didn't have the energy to end it. Beth looked after me and took me to see the doctor. He put me back on anti-depressants and told me that I would have to take them for the rest of my life. Beth was instructed to give me my meds and to take me for a walk everyday. We settled in to a routine of medication, videos and silence. It suited both of us fine.

One day, like all the other days, we walked to the library to get movies. I had been off work for several weeks so we had already watched most of the videos at the small library. Beth picked up one of the few movies I hadn't seen and asked if I wanted to watch it. I said I didn't care, which was my standard answer for everything. The movie was called 'Jesus'.

Chapter Four

"The Lord is my light and my salvation—whom shall I fear?"

Psalm 27:1

Beth was not interested in watching the movie so I sat alone in the living room. I had no hope or expectation about the movie, or, for that matter, anything else. I stared at the screen because it was on. At the end of the movie a narrator did a brief teaching on salvation and invited viewers to join him in a prayer. I was accustomed to praying to God (as I understood Him) through my 12-step training. I knelt down on the floor and said the prayer after the narrator, inviting Jesus to become the Lord of my life.

And He did.

The room immediately filled with light and it felt like wind was rushing around me and then through me. The weight of all of the sins I had ever committed landed on me and I thought I would be crushed. Emotional pain shot through my body as the lightening of truth illuminated my life and exposed my sin. I felt like I was being physically pushed through the floor and I thought the pain itself might kill me. I was crying uncontrollably as waves of quilt and shame crashed over me.

Suddenly, in a moment, all of the weight and pain and sin were lifted from me. I felt like I had been purified by God's love. It was as if someone had ripped the shirt off my back, so complete was the removal. I could feel the presence of the Lord, as if the light was radiating love. Peace filled my heart and I began to weep tears of joy. I heard a voice in my heart and I knew it was Jesus. He told me two things that day: that I was to build His church, and that we were going to do something about this lifestyle. I told Him that if He would lead me, I would follow Him anywhere. My life changed that moment. Everything I had ever done was washed away. Jesus answered my prayer, filled my heart and became my Lord and Savior.

Chapter Five

*"...continue to work out your salvation with fear
and trembling, for it is God who works in you to will
and to act according to His good purpose."*

Philippians 2:12–13

When God shows up, He shows up. My depression was replaced, that moment, by pure peace. I was no longer afraid, no longer withdrawn and I was anything but quiet. The only thing I wanted to do was to talk to people about Jesus. I wanted everyone to know Him, so that they could feel the peace and joy that I felt. I wanted to share the Good News with everyone I talked to. What I quickly learned was that not everyone was as excited about my new life as I was.

Within hours of me being born-again in the living room, Beth took me to my mother's house. Everyone was at a loss of what to do with me. Instead of my depressed, sullen self, I was happy, excited and more talkative than I had been in my life. I tried to explain to Mom what had happened, but all I got was raised eyebrows and 'okay dear'. They asked me to sit on the couch while they discussed things in the kitchen. I didn't care; I was free. I asked Mom if she had a Bible. She rummaged around until she finally located it. I immediately started reading the Word, hungry to know more about this Jesus. I was completely in love with God and all I wanted was more of Him.

My sister walked through the door a short while later. I knew that she had been called in for this 'family crisis'. She waved at me and went straight to the kitchen. I could hear them talking about manic phases, drug interactions and the psych ward. I knew that they were contemplating a short-term lock up. My sister being there turned out to be a Godsend.

Brenda had gotten saved a couple years earlier in the waiting room of a children's hospital in Virginia. Her newborn son was in neo-natal ICU, fighting to stay alive. She had called the nurse's desk to be buzzed in, as she had several times a day since his birth. Instead of a courteous "Thank you, come on in", she was instructed to wait at the door, as a doctor was coming to speak to her momentarily. Brenda had worked as a volunteer Emergency Medical Technician. She knew that doctors seldom came to speak to a parent with good news. Before the doctor arrived Brenda's husband walked around the corner. It was obvious that he had been crying. He looked at her, shook his head and then walked away.

Brenda later told me that she was certain that Nicholas was gone. She said she felt her legs give out and she grabbed for the railing on the wall. She missed the railing but just before she hit the floor she felt someone catch her. She felt herself being steadied back to her feet, strong arms gently lifting her from behind. She thought it must have been the doctor, but when she turned around to thank him there was no one there. She told me that she knew it was an angel, that she could feel his presence and his warmth. Momentarily the doctor came out and told her that one of Nicholas' lungs had collapsed, but they had been able to re-inflate it and stabilize him. Nicholas was alive and Brenda was born-again.

After much discussion about what to do with me, my sister convinced Mom and Beth that I would be fine and did not need to be locked up. As the days turned to weeks I often went to Brenda for reassurance. I needed to be reminded that I hadn't, in fact, lost my mind. She continually told me that God was more real than anybody knew, and that if He had told me to do something, then I should do it.

It took quite a while for my family to adapt to my new life. My hunger for God and His Word seemed to increase daily. People politely asked me, and then told me, to quit talking to them about God. So I tried to talk more to God, than about Him and continued to study the Bible.

I decided that if I was to build His church then I should learn how to build. I didn't know at the time that He was not referring to a physical structure, so I quit my job at the factory and became an apprentice carpenter. I went back to the church that I had attended as a child. I knew nothing about religion, doctrines or beliefs. I thought that all churches served the same God, and that they were all alike. I've since learned that's not true.

I was building houses, going to church and reading the Bible everyday. Something disconcerting started to happen. The more I read, the less comfortable I was in my life. I read the scriptures in Leviticus and Romans, and tried to overlook them. I tried to ignore the conviction that came over me when I read passages that condemned homosexuality. I tried to justify my life with the teachings from the gay church I used to attend. I tried, but it never quite stuck. My life, or should I say my sin, was no longer comfortable.

God was so faithful to reveal Himself to me during my times of study. I was fascinated by the stories I read and awed by God's power to deliver. I had always suspected that there was a god; I just didn't know that He loved me. The more I read the more I wanted to read. I was enraptured by His character.

Because I read so much, I started to notice things in my church that didn't line up with the Word. I was one of those 'all zeal, no wisdom' people, so I continually asked my pastor why we weren't doing things the way God told us to. He was patient and kind, but couldn't provide answers that suited me.

I had the opportunity to do a couple of mission trips (much to the chagrin of my church) and met some Spirit-filled believers that opened my eyes to the possibility of something more. My faith increased and God started using me to do some wild things. It was pretty amazing.

As my relationship with God grew, my home life crumbled. The conviction of my lifestyle weighed heavily upon me, but not at all on my partner. Beth couldn't understand what had happened to me. I couldn't blame her, because I didn't understand it either. I was unable to explain how I went from a card-carrying lesbian to a Jesus freak who only wanted more of God. We tried to return to our 'normal' life, but I struggled at every turn. I was still attracted to her, I was still in love with her, but I couldn't be the person that I was before. We went and talked to the pastor about our marriage problem since it was no secret that she and I were together. I tried to tell him about Leviticus and Romans and how I felt weird about being with her. He told me that God was love and, since we loved each other, that God was in our relationship. He told me that I was born a lesbian and would always be a lesbian…just as God had intended. Every time we left a counseling session my partner was excited and I was confused. I knew enough of the Bible to know that the priests were supposed to know what was going on, and that we were to obey what the man of God said. I tried very hard to maintain my marriage and to be a good spouse, but every time I read those scriptures my heart hurt again.

I wasn't convinced that the counsel I was receiving lined up with God's Word. It occurred to me that perhaps the pastor had some personal reasons for not wanting to examine the scriptures too closely. I asked him if he could refer us to another Christian who could counsel us. He complied and gave us the name of a counselor in a nearby city. Beth and I attended sessions with her and tried to straighten out our relationship (no pun intended).

It was this counselor that erroneously explained the quarrelsome scriptures to me in detail. I was particularly hung up on Romans 1:20-32, part of which discusses how "women exchanged the natural use for what is against nature". It goes on to discuss male homosexuality and sexual immorality. I couldn't understand why, if being gay was okay, God would tell us not to do it. The counselor explained it to me as follows: if a straight woman were to have sex with another female, that would be going against her nature. For a straight woman, her nature is to have sex with a man. Likewise, since I was a homosexual, my nature is to have sex with a woman. For me to have sex with a man I would be going against my nature and it would therefore be an abomination to God. She assured me that God knew what He was doing when He made me and that He meant for me to be gay. That lie, combined with several others, allowed me to stay trapped in my sin for another year. I thank God for His continued mercy and grace.

Here's the thing about God: if you're really seeking Him and His truth, He will reveal Himself to you. It didn't matter that everyone that I talked to agreed with my partner. It didn't matter that everyone I knew thought I was wrong. It didn't even matter that I lost most of my friends and family when I became a Christian. I only wanted God, and that was enough.

We settled into an uneasy truce about our marriage. I tried hard not to Jesus-ify everything and she tried hard to figure out what to do with the new me. It seemed obvious that I was the one who was deceived, as everyone around us told me to settled down and honor the marriage vows that I had made before God. It was a daily struggle.

I kept crying out in my prayer time for God to change me into the woman he intended me to be. I didn't know what that was, but I knew He could do it. God answers prayers, sometimes in bizarre ways.

Chapter Six

*"...He has sent me to bind up the brokenhearted, to
proclaim freedom for the captives..."*

Isaiah 61:1

My real freedom began in September of that year. By this time it had been more than two years since Jesus had shown up in my living room. I was still living with Beth and doing my best to be a good spouse.

Beth had a 12-step sponsee named Penny. She had been having trouble with bad dreams and night terrors and had somehow gotten connected to a pastor that claimed to know something about spiritual warfare. At this time I knew nothing about deliverance, other than what I had read in the Bible. This pastor was supposed to be coming to her house to help her with the nightmares. Beth was going over to support her sponsee during this meeting. I wasn't at work that day because I had been off due to a bronchial infection. For some reason, Beth called me and asked if I wanted to come over for lunch. She said that Penny was a little nervous about meeting this pastor and wondered if I would come over. I said okay, imagining tuna salad, cookies and fruit punch. We all got more than we bargained for.

Lunch was pleasant and uneventful, and then the pastor and his wife arrived. I knew the pastor because I used to drink and do drugs with his son. I hadn't seen him in years, but he remembered me and told me that I used to go to tent meetings with him when I was very young. I have no recollection of tent meetings, but that's neither here nor there. We moved into the living room and the pastor talked to Penny about Jesus, the cross and salvation. I was quite amazed, as the pastor knew the entire Bible by memory. Penny would ask questions about God and Jesus and the Holy Ghost, and Pastor Jim would tell her where to find the answer in the Bible. Hold on now, because this is where it got crazy.

Beth was typically very cordial and polite. She was not antagonistic or given to fits of sarcasm. That day, however, she was completely off the chain. She was mildly aggressive towards the pastor and borderline rude. She challenged him at every turn and was generally disagreeable. Pastor Jim handled it politely and eventually led Penny to the Lord through a prayer of salvation.

About the time the pastor and his wife rose to leave, Beth asked a very pointed question about homosexuality. Pastor Jim responded by saying that that conversation was very long, and better suited for another time. She persisted and asked him if the Bible said it was wrong. Pastor Jim took a deep breath and said yes. Then she asked him if he thought homosexuals went to hell. Again he said yes. Somewhere amid the deep breaths and the hostile questions, Pastor Jim asked Beth if he could pray for her. Her defenses dropped, momentarily, and she said yes. Then she went back to twenty questions. Eventually the pastor and his wife decided it was time to pray for her. I had been watching this whole thing, frankly surprised at Beth's demeanor and behavior. Pastor Jim asked Beth to stand in front of him and he had his wife stand beside him. I was sitting on the loveseat and the newly born-again sponsee was on the couch.

When they started praying I closed my eyes and lifted my hands. I often pray with my hands raised, like a sign of surrender. As they were praying, something very weird happened. It felt like someone grabbed me by the forearms and was trying to pull my arms backwards. I had my eyes closed and didn't know what was going on, so I tried to pull my arms down in front of me. The harder I tried, the more pressure was on my arms. The pull was so intense that it felt like my shoulders we're being pulled out of joint. I tried to pull forward and I was pushed off of the loveseat and onto the floor. I felt like I was picked up from behind and then dropped to the floor. I was on my knees and being pulled (seemingly from behind) onto my back. I heard voices but they were very muffled and very far away. It sounded like there was crashing water all around me. The more I struggled, the further back my arms were pulled. Something in my chest popped and it was very painful. From far away I heard Pastor Jim saying "Loose her, in Jesus' name. Loose her, in Jesus' name." A series of pictures flashed across my mind, much like a collection of snapshots viewed very quickly. In each picture was the face of a man who had abused me. After the snapshots flashed through, Pastor Jim's voice got clearer and the crashing waves went away. I heard him say, "In the name of Jesus I command you to loose her." My arms were released and they fell forward. I was on the floor, very scared and with a very bad pain in my chest. Pastor Jim was standing with one hand on my partner and one stretched towards me. His wife was standing in front of me. I opened my eyes and she offered her hand to me to help me up. She told me to stand up and praise Jesus, so I did.

I looked around the room and tried to figure out what happened. It felt like my chest had been opened with a pry bar. It was quiet, except for the pastor and his wife thanking God. Penny cleared her throat and said, "Um, what was that?"

Pastor Jim explained that, through the power of Jesus, a demon had just been cast out of me. I didn't know anything about demons except what I had read in the Bible. I certainly didn't know I had any. My partner asked why, when he was praying for her, the demon came out of me. Pastor Jim explained that, because we were involved sexually, 'the two became one flesh'. To Satan, she and I were the same person. Therefore, when she got prayer to get set free, the demon manifested. It just happened to come out through me.

That was the day I was set free from the spirit of homo-sexuality.

Chapter Seven

"Watch and pray so that you do not fall into temptation. The spirit is willing, but the body is weak."

Matthew 26:41

L iving in deception is relatively easy, because you are deceived. You don't question behaviors, motives or thoughts; you just plod along and subconsciously try to avoid the truth. Once the deception is brought into the light by truth, then the real work begins.

The day I was delivered from homosexuality I had to tell Beth that I could no longer be with her. Because of the codependency in our relationship, it took a good while to sort out the details of what 'not being together' meant. It happened for me in stages. I did not have sex with her again, but I couldn't figure out where to draw the line regarding other contact. We had slept in the same bed for 10 years, so it was hard moving to another room. It was hard not kissing her goodnight and it was hard not saying 'I love you'. The demon was gone, but the habits and feelings were not. My road to freedom was very long and very painful.

The separation process started with the material things. We sold our home and moved into a two-bedroom apartment in a triplex that we owned. Looking back, we should have separated immediately, but hindsight is always 20/20. I thought,

somehow, we could continue to be friends and business partners, but not lovers. She thought that if she waited me out, I
would eventually come to my senses and we would get our life
back. Neither one of us were right. We entered an awkward
and painful phase of trying to be a non-sexual couple. I still
went to work and built houses while she looked after the
house and had dinner waiting for me when I got home. We
still did everything together except have sex. I would like to
tell you that I was never tempted, but that's a lie. Thankfully,
by God's grace, every time one of us tried to cross the line,
conviction would fall on me like a meteor. I can't tell you how
many times God saved me from backsliding into that lifestyle
again.

The next several months would be some of the hardest
days I have ever known. I had lived as a lesbian for seventeen
years, my entire adult life. I had lived with Beth for over half
of that time. I learned very quickly that the flesh cares nothing about spiritual matters; it only wants to be fed. It is not
interested in doing what is right, what is holy or what is pleas-
ing to God. The flesh is only interested in carnal matters like
food, sex and satisfaction. My flesh did not die a quick or
quiet death.

My family took the news almost as bad as Beth. Our
close-knit circle of friends quietly chose Beth's side and, for
the most part, cut me out of their lives. My dearest friend, who
had been the 'best man' at my wedding, told me that I was a
Jesus freak and that she was looking for a new best friend. I
was devastated. It was a horribly lonely and confusing time.

I started attending Pastor Jim's church the week after I
had been delivered. Within days I received the Baptism of the
Holy Spirit with the evidence of speaking in tongues. I continued to study the Word and pray every day. I firmly believe
that it was only the grace of God that carried me through that
incredibly dark and lonely time.

A funny thing happened a short while before my deliverance. Beth had started watching a lady preacher on television and was always trying to get me to watch her. I didn't like TV evangelists, but Beth started taping the show and playing it during dinner. At first I could barely tolerate it, but then I really got to like it. The teaching was solid and I didn't hear her say anything that didn't line up with the Word. As time passed, Beth and I both started watching her on a daily basis.

A couple of months after my deliverance, Beth told me that she thought I was supposed to get a job working for this woman's ministry. Now, this particular ministry is one of the largest media ministries in the world and this woman is known in Christian circles worldwide. The idea of working for her seemed about as feasible as me calling up NASA and asking if I could pilot the next space shuttle. I told Beth that I thought she was nuts. I also couldn't fathom us living apart. We were physically separated, but still very much enmeshed. We still went everywhere together, did everything together and, for the most part, still had the life we had had for the past 10 years.

I walked everyday and prayed. We lived a few blocks north of the river so everyday I would walk to the river and pray. I didn't know what I was supposed to do. I was doing my best to follow what I was reading in the Word. I had joined Pastor Jim's church and was involved in whatever they were doing. I was tithing, attending Bible studies and reading the Word daily. I wanted to know God. I wanted Him to show up and talk to me like He did before. I wanted so badly to make Him happy.

In an effort to sort out some of my confusion I went and stayed with the only Christian friends I had at the time. I had met this couple in Jamaica on a mission trip and again in Mexico. Cindy was the woman I had called after my deliverance, desperately seeking answers. She and her husband allowed me to come and stay with them for a few days while I tried to sort through the chaos. I felt like my entire existence was teetering on the brink of insanity. Everything that I had believed to be true was unraveling. I was a wreck. I told Cindy that I needed God to tell me something; to give me direction. She told me that if I asked Him to speak to me, maybe He would. We prayed together and asked God to give me a word. The following day I was alone at their house and I was lying on the couch. I had fallen asleep while reading the Bible. I was awakened by a male voice. I jumped up, thinking that Cindy's husband had come home. I listened but didn't hear anyone moving around. I called out 'hello?' but no one answered. I sat down on the couch. I heard the voice again, this time very clearly. All He said was "Wait." That was the first time I had heard God's voice audibly. Had I known He was really going to speak to me, I would have asked Him for more than a word. When Cindy got home I told her what had happened and she cried. At the time I didn't know that not everyone hears His voice. A few days later I returned home and tried to wait. I didn't know what I was waiting for, but I knew that was what He had asked me to do.

Beth and I were struggling to figure out our own identities. She ran hot and cold with church, and I ran hotter and hotter. I pleaded with God to change me, and He complied.

Three months after I had been delivered from homosexuality, God started dealing with me about going to work for the TV evangelist. I was so busy asking Him to show me the way that I didn't have time to listen to His instructions. It has been my experience that God always deals with me privately. It's only when I don't heed private correction that He takes my business public. He had told me to apply to that ministry and I told Him no. I thought that my 'no' was justifiable as Beth was still sick, we still had this apartment building to look after and I still had to go to work. Because of my disobedience God started closing doors. I got laid off from my job, but that didn't seem like a big deal because I was often laid off during the winter. The difference this time was that I couldn't get another job. I couldn't get factory work, temp work, or even a place to volunteer. It was like I could hear God slamming the doors shut. By December I was desperate for work, squirming in my disobedience and thoroughly unhappy with my life. I have since discovered that there is no comfort in disobedience, only prolonged misery.

By the third week of December I was willing to do anything. A friend of my mother's had asked me to fill in for her for a couple of overnight shifts. My job was to make sure that the elderly gentleman I was watching got to the bathroom and back safely during the night. Sounds easy, right? The tricky part was that he got up about every forty-five minutes, seldom knew who I was, and almost always peed on the floor. And, as an added bonus, sometimes his medicine made him a little hostile.

During one of those long nights, I was reading a magazine from that TV evangelist's ministry. On the back cover was a small ad that said they were looking for people to come and work for them. I was shocked. I prayed about it, still not wanting to leave, but knowing that anything had to be better that spending my nights mopping up around the toilet. I decided to send in an application. I mailed it in, waited a week and then did a follow-up call. I was fully expecting (and hoping) that they would tell me the positions were already filled. I still didn't want to move, but the price of disobedience was weighing heavily on me. I wanted to obey God by sending in the application, and then I wanted God to honor my obedience by not making me go. God always has a plan, and it has seldom lined up with mine.

I made the call and was told that because I lived in Canada I could not be considered for a position in their US office. I thanked them for their time and secretly celebrated that I didn't have to go. About a week later I was doing another endless overnight and I read an article about an internship program at one of her outreaches. As it turned out, not only did this woman preach the gospel around the world, she also sponsored an inner-city church in the Mid-west. And, she sponsored a free, 4–12 month internship for people who wanted to learn more about full-time ministry. Twelve months I knew I couldn't do, but the four-month deal sounded like a good idea. After all, it's not like I'd be leaving Beth, just going away to work for a couple of months. Justification is a two-way street. The problem now was that the internship started about ten days from the time I heard about it. That meant I had to get the application, gather all the paperwork, get the recommendation letters and get it back to them practically yesterday. There was no way I could get it done in time. The lesson I learned here was that God can open doors as easily as He can shut them.

I was brutally honest on the application. They asked questions about drugs and alcohol and abuse. They asked about sex and cigarettes and witchcraft. It looked like I was batting a thousand as the checkmarks continued to build. I realized that there was no possible way, based on the application, that any church would want me to do anything for them. Since I thought that that might be my out, I told them all the gory details of my life. It was quite an application. I faxed it to them and waited for my rejection letter.

The deadline was closing in. In fact, it was down to the point that, if I was accepted, I had to leave that day. I had bought new clothes (that met the ministry dress code) and new luggage. I left the tags on all of it because I knew that if they rejected me I was going back to building houses. I got the call about 10am. They had accepted me. I left for the Mid-west that afternoon. I had no idea that sixteen hours away was a new world.

Chapter Eight

"Therefore, if anyone is in Christ, he is a new creation; old things have passed away; behold, all things have become new."

2 Corinthians 5:17

It snowed almost the whole way there. I drove through a whiteout and watched a tractor-trailer roll over in front of me. There were dozens of wrecks and traffic was horrible. I questioned my choice and my sanity every hundred miles or so. What on earth was I doing? I didn't know a single person in the state I was driving to, and I was quite sure I didn't want to. I had no idea how I was going to support myself and I didn't know for sure that I could even exist without Beth. I was a mess.

I had been worried about finances when I was contemplating the move. I knew that the Bible said I wasn't supposed to worry about what I was going to eat or what I was going to wear. I knew that, but I worried anyway. A couple of days before I got accepted I gave God an ultimatum. (Just for the record, that is never a good idea). I told Him that if He wanted me to go, that He had to send me money that day. He spoke to my spirit and said "Don't test Me, child." I told God, "Oh, I'm testing You, and if You don't send me money in the mail today, I'm not going." I went to the post office that afternoon and got a check in the mail. It was payable to Donna Frank and the amount was one cent. I looked at the check and heard God laugh. As it turned out I had over paid an insurance policy and they were returning the difference. Nobody can tell me that God doesn't have a sense of humor.

At one point during the drive the snow changed to rain for a short while. I was asking God to show me a sign that it was Him that had sent me. Suddenly everything around me turned pink: the road, the concrete barriers, everything. I looked in my rearview mirror and saw that most beautiful red sunset that I've ever seen. The sun was reflecting off the rain so everything had a pink glow. It was breathtaking. It soothed my soul, at least for the moment. God has always showed up for me in my midnight hour, even when midnight comes at sunset.

I arrived at the inner-city church right at noon. I don't know what I expected, but it wasn't that. They politely told me that the pastor I needed to speak with had gone to lunch. The first hour at my new home was spent in a plastic chair beside the reception window. As it neared 1pm a group of young people (young compared to me) gathered at the foot of a stairwell about 20 feet from me. I first noticed a tall guy acting goofy and an obnoxious woman in an orange sweatshirt. I decided immediately that whoever they were, we would not spend time together. As you may have guessed, they turned out to be my fellow interns and we would spend the next year living and working together. The loud one in the sweatshirt was talking about some older lady that was supposed to be coming as an intern. She supposed that the old woman would try to mother them all and she wasn't looking forward to that. I didn't realize that I was the old woman they were referring to until they were deep into the conversation. I paid them absolutely no attention, but entertained myself by plotting their demise. Shortly thereafter a friendly young pastor introduced himself to me and then introduced me to the group at the bottom of the stairs.

So, there I was; a thousand miles from everyone I knew, and a million miles from where I wanted to be. Had I known then what would be required of me, I very likely would have climbed back into my pickup and drove home.

I got settled in for my four-month journey. They assigned me a roommate a couple of weeks after I'd arrived and I was forced to share my 10'X10' room with a woman I didn't know who snored horribly and slept the majority of the time. Prior to her arrival, I had occupied my non-working time by either doing my assignments or locking myself in my room. Since she was almost always in her bed, I was forced to venture out.

As interns we were kept very busy. We had classes, homework, outreaches and job placements. We generally had to be somewhere by at least 8am and worked everyday except Monday. You would think that with all that activity my brain would line up or my body would shut down. Neither happened.

I didn't know what to do at night so I drove my truck around the city. I was afraid to stay and afraid to leave. I spoke to Beth almost daily. We had all the struggles of a long-distance relationship with none of the benefits. We continued to feed off of each other's fears and weaknesses. We continued to expect that somehow, God would bless our unholy 'friendship'. It was excruciating.

After being there for a couple of months, some rather bizarre things started happening in the residence. A construction crew from Texas was also being housed there and, based on the cigarette butts and empty beer cans, I suspect they were predominantly unsaved. A lot of us that lived there started getting headaches. People would feel like someone was watching them but when they turned around no one would be there. I remember sitting in my room (my roommate had left the program shortly after she arrived) doing homework, and the temperature dropping several degrees in a matter of seconds. It was weird. One day in class our instructor, Pastor Walker, was talking about the things that were going on. We were sitting with the lights out and he was wearing sunglasses because of his headache. He asked what we thought was going on in the residence. Someone suggested that there might be a demon there. He asked the class what we thought and how we should get rid of it. I told him, intending it to be a joke, that it lived in my room. My head was pounding so hard that I thought it might actually explode.

"Pastor, what would happen, hypothetically, if the demon lived in one of us?" I couldn't believe that I had asked the question out loud.

Something inside me snapped when he said, "Donna, do you want to deal with this now?"

I didn't know what was happening, but I felt a tear slide down my cheek. I was sitting with my head on the table because it was hurting so bad. Carol, the intern with the orange sweatshirt, was sitting at the table in front of me, and Matt, an introverted guy with very little to say was sitting beside me. Pastor Walker had moved around the room and was now behind me. I don't know what he said but when he spoke I jumped up from the table and stood with my back against the wall, ready to fight. I had no idea that I was man-ifesting. I felt like something in my mind had slid sideways. It was like I was watching myself on a movie screen but didn't get to decide what I said or did. I could hear a voice inside of me telling me very wicked things. It was instructing me how to hurt Carol and Matt. I should probably point out that Carol, Matt and I had become, at least superficially, friends. The voice within me told me that I should destroy them.

At the same time though, there was another voice that was telling me to get everyone out of the room. I could hear the voices fighting in my head, and I was afraid to speak because I didn't know which one was in control of my mouth. As calmly as I could I said, "I'm not feeling very well and I think you guys need to leave." The voice in my head was screaming at me not to let them get away. Someone from the back of the room suggested that they pray for me. Pastor Walker had left the room to go find help. Carol had left her table, ran to the back of the room and said, "She wants us out, I'm leaving. Y'all can stay if you want to but I'm outta here."

I'm not sure how long I stood there, listening to the voices and watching the movie. The interns left and staff members started walking into the room. I watched several pastors walk in, and with each one the dark voice laughed louder. The last person to walk in was a woman who had moved to our state just a couple of weeks after I had. All I knew about her was that her name was Miss Alliece and that she managed the women's rehab home, along with several other departments. When she walked into the room the voice that had been laughing at the pastors stopped cold. I don't know if it came out verbally or not, but the voice said, "All you other people can stay, but she has got to go". She just grinned at me. I didn't know her very well at all but the spirits within me certainly recognized her. I ran into the corner and tried to hide behind a plastic tree. The pastors spread out across the room. If any of them were talking, I didn't hear them. All I could hear was Miss Alliece saying, "Donna. Donna. Donna." She said it so softly and with so much compassion that I wanted to scream. I moved across the room to get away from her. As I walked past the windows I contemplated whether I could jump out the window and run away without being caught. I decided that even if I got through both panes of glass, I would probably break something in the fall. Please keep in mind that throughout this whole experience, I feel like I'm watching a bad movie and can't shut it off. The voices are screaming in my head to find a way out and to avoid, at all costs, Miss Alliece.

I kept walking around the room and was almost to the door. There was a pulpit at the front of the room. I don't know if somebody hit it or if it just fell, but it came crashing to the ground. Everyone turned to see what happened and I lunged for the door. I couldn't get it opened before one of the pastors

grabbed me and pulled me back from it. A struggle ensued
and much of the next several minutes is a blur. I ended up sitting under a table against the back wall. I had lost my shoes
and I had bruises up and down my arms and legs where people had tried to restrain me. One of the pastors was trying to
talk to me under the table. Miss Alliece, still as calm and as
gentle as the moment she walked in, suggested that they move
the table so they could better talk to me. Once the table was
moved, the pastor started asking me questions. I wanted to
talk, and I very badly wanted help, but the dark voices inside
were still in full control. For a while I couldn't say anything,
and then I started cussing at the pastors and saying filthy
things to them. In my mind I was screaming at myself to shut
up, but the profanity just kept coming. Eventually the pastor
told me I couldn't speak to him like that because he was a man
of God. I quit speaking entirely for several minutes, until he
wanted me to confess Jesus Christ as Lord. I repeated everything that he wanted me to say, and the voice inside just
laughed. The pastors looked around, visibly relieved, and
acted like they were done. I was unable to speak and terrified
that they were going to leave me like that. I had studied the
Bible enough to know that if a demon is cast out and the house
is not filled, it will return with seven demons more wicked
than itself. I wanted to scream out, "Help me, there's more
here!" but I was unable to speak.

The pastors were getting up, straightening their ties and
all but high-fiving each other. I just sat there, apparently looking quite delivered. Miss Alliece looked at me and then at the
pastors. She said, "It's still here, I can taste it."

She sat down on the floor a few feet away from me. She
started praying in tongues and I immediately smashed my
head against the block wall I was leaning on. She kept praying
and I smashed my head again. She stopped praying long
enough to ask the pastor that was closest to me to move me
away from the wall. He grabbed my feet and dragged me a

few feet towards the center of the room. Miss Alliece continued to pray and it felt like my entire soul was being ripped from bottom to top. I don't know if I yelled out loud, but from within my spirit a blood-curdling scream came up from my toes. I felt like I was being turned inside out.

Then, it left.

I sat there, not really knowing what had happened. The movie had ended and I was pretty sure I was able to talk again. Miss Alliece smiled at me and started singing softly. I crawled across the floor and laid my head in her lap. She continued to sing and she put her hand on my head. It was the safest I had ever felt in my life, and I cried. I don't know how long I stayed there, but she continued to sing that heavenly song.

Eventually I sat up and dried my eyes. She told me that she wanted to explain what had happened and what I should expect. She told me that the demons had been cast out but that they would revisit and try to get back in. She said it was like they were in the yard, but they wanted to be in the house. She told me that they would knock on the door and pound on the windows. She told me it was my job to keep them out. She told me that the only way they could get back in was if I opened a door.

At the time I didn't understand anything about spiritual warfare or legal access. I had only ever heard about two deliverances in my life, and I was at the center of both of them. I was grateful for the teaching, and terrified that they would come back. They have tried to revisit repeatedly, but that simple teaching has kept me free. Miss Alliece told me that when they knock on the door to say, "In the name of Jesus I command you to leave". I decided that I would always send Jesus to answer the door.

Here's the thing about deliverance; most people think that the hard part is getting free. My experience has been that the hard part is staying free. It's kind of like getting sober. I was always able to stop drinking; I just had a problem staying stopped. It's the same with deliverance. You can have everyone you know binding and loosing and rebuking and casting, but if you don't walk out your own deliverance, you're not going to stay free. Deliverance closes the doors that had allowed Satan legal access to your soul. It's your job to keep the doors closed.

Chapter Nine

*"He made himself to bore our sins in his body on
the tree, so that we might die to sins and live for
righteousness; by his wounds you have been
healed."*

1 Peter 2:24

I really thought that after I had manifested (twice) and had
demons cast out of me (twice), that my life would get easier. It got significantly harder. I no longer had the deception to hide behind, so the naked truth of my brokenness came
to the forefront. It sounds crazy, but there is some comfort in
being blinded by demonic oppression. There is a counterfeit
form of freedom that feels like liberty. When large parts of my
life and thinking were being directed by evil forces, it was relatively easy for me to sit back. Puppeteering is not hard for the
puppet, but it's a lot of work for the one holding the strings.
Any time we allow Satan to be in charge of any part of our
mind, will or emotions, we become a puppet for the dark side.
The only way to cut those strings is with the power of Jesus
Christ.

There were a number of areas in my life that needed to be
overhauled by God. I can't take any credit for the victory; God
truly did all the work for me. I have found that the only thing
God requires of me is willingness. In some of the really tough
areas, like forgiving people that had abused me, I wasn't even

able to offer Him willingness. But, I was willing to be willing. All God needs is our agreement. It's not by power or by might that we are delivered, but by His Spirit.

Some of my areas of struggle are listed here, along with some of the tools that helped me overcome. I have also compiled a list of books that were instrumental in my healing, which can be found at the back of this book. I encourage you to know your weaknesses and to know your God. I believe this can only be accomplished through careful study of both.

Lust

One of the hardest areas for me to maintain my freedom was in the area of lust. In almost every relationship I struggled with infidelity. In fact, prior to my marriage I had never managed to stay faithful. I was continually fighting thoughts, even when I felt that I really loved the person I was with. I felt horrible about my behavior but I didn't know how to stop it. After my first deliverance I learned that I wasn't supposed to be physically involved with anyone unless it was within the marriage covenant. That created a definite problem for me, so I searched for other avenues of release. At one point someone loaned me a book that said fantasizing and self-gratification were the equivalent of having sex with demons. Given my history of deliverance, I knew I didn't need to be messing around with that. The day that I read that book I repented to God and asked Him to free me from unholy behaviors. Immediately, He did just that.

What I discovered about lust was that it all started in my head. 1 John 2:16 talks about the lust of the flesh, the lust of the eyes and the pride of life. The flesh craves satisfaction, at any cost. The lust of the flesh is often fuelled by what our eyes take in and today's media offers a virtual buffet of unholy sights. By starting to monitor what I was taking in through my eyes the thoughts became easier to tame. Since lust had started in my mind, that's where I had to stop it.

Mind/Thoughts

The physical side of freedom turned out to be an easier dog to leash than the mental deviance. My mind was a pit. My conversations were filthy and I didn't know how to clean them up. Every time I opened my mouth I spewed perversion. That had been my life. Anyone who has spent any time in the gay community knows how sex-based it is. It seems that everybody has dated everybody else, or is planning to. It is expected that you'll stay friends with your ex, because you know you'll be seeing him or her at the Christmas party. I seldom saw healing after breakups because there was never time to grieve. Everybody just dusted themselves off, called their friends and made a plan to meet their next ex, hopefully before whoever just dumped them found theirs. It was a vicious cycle of rejection and replacement.

I heard something in church one day that changed my life. I had been trying to be a 'good person' and to think 'clean thoughts' but I was failing miserably. I tried, when I had perverse thoughts, to think pure thoughts instead. It didn't work. Then my pastor said that it's impossible to fight a thought with a thought; that thoughts can only be fought with the Word of God. That simple truth changed my life. It didn't stop the thoughts from coming, but it did give me a weapon to fight them with. Philippians 4:8 became my mantra. Every time that lust, wickedness or perversion tried to enter my head I repeated that scripture. "Finally, brothers, whatever is true, whatever is noble, whatever is right, whatever is pure, whatever is lovely, whatever is admirable—if anything is excellent or praiseworthy—think about such things." The only one I knew that was all of those things was Jesus. I found it was difficult to think about immorality and Jesus at the same time. As always, light prevailed over darkness.

I eventually learned how to take thoughts captive to the obedience of Christ Jesus. This was by no means an overnight process, as I had been programmed, from childhood, to operate from a sex-based nature. The homosexuality I entered at age 17 was just a continuation of the perversion I had grown up in. As a born-again, Spirit-filled believer, I struggled daily with seemingly endless unholy thoughts. Hopefully not everyone will have to walk the walk that I did, but I know that right now some of you are thinking about sex as you're trying to focus on these words. The good news is, there is freedom for you too. God is no respecter of person; what He'll do for one He'll do for another. I carried Scriptures around in my pockets to keep me on track. I wore WWJD (What Would Jesus Do) bracelets and a ring on my wedding finger that said 'Pray Hard'. I prayed everyday that God would purify my mind and burn those thoughts from me. It has been an arduous process, but God continues to be faithful. We submit to God, resist the devil, and he must flee (James 4:7).

Mouth

The next area I had to work on was my mouth. I managed to quit cursing almost immediately after being saved, but I had a problem with grumbling, complaining and negativity. I could be cuttingly sarcastic and I often hurt people without meaning to. It was like my mind and my mouth were complete strangers. It seemed that if a thought came into my head it immediately flew out of my mouth without ever checking with my brain. It was maddening.

The Book of Proverbs has helped me a lot in this area, as it offers a lot of wisdom about when to speak and what to say. I try to read a chapter from Proverbs every day as part of my daily study. Since there are thirty-one proverbs, I usually read the one that matches the date. For example, if it is the fifth day of the month, I read Proverbs 5. This practice has helped me both with my thought life and my mouth. One of my personal favorites is Proverbs 17:28 "Even a fool is thought wise if he keeps silent, and discerning if he holds his tongue." This continues to be a work in progress, as I often still open my mouth and prove myself a fool. God's grace however, is sufficient.

Guarding the Gates

Another area that I think is very important is learning to guard the gates. The Bible tells us that we are to guard our hearts, and the way we do that is by guarding the gates. I didn't understand what that meant so I asked God what the gates were to my heart. He told me that they were every opening in my body. I had to think that through, but it made a lot of sense. If you have an eight-foot fence around your property, the only easy (and legal) way in is through a gate. The gates I have to guard are my eyes, ears, nose, mouth, and those openings south of the beltline. I don't mean to be vulgar, but it's the truth that sets us free.

I guard my eyes by turning them from evil things. In today's society this is a never-ending battle. I try very hard not to watch anything that is vulgar or profane. I don't watch programs or movies that glorify sex outside of marriage and I don't 'check out' people as I'm walking down the street. I try to protect my eyes from anything that could affect my heart. If you're thinking 'She must not watch much of anything', you're right. I watch very little secular television and I seldom watch movies that are rated higher than PG-13. It took me weeks and months and years to get free from the perversity of my thinking. Hollywood has not yet made a movie good enough for me to risk that freedom.

I have similar standards with what I listen to; almost no secular music, no vulgar comedians or commentaries, and no talk shows that glorify evil. I am very grateful for the almost endless supply of Christian music and teaching tapes that are available. Out of the abundance of the heart the mouth speaks (Matthew 12:34). I want my abundance to be praise.

Thousands of dollars were spent during my cocaine addiction. I don't ever want to forget to protect what goes into my body through my nose. I don't want to give the devil any room for temptation through what I smell; whether it's a familiar perfume, a favorite drink, or a puff of weed. It's important to guard the gates, regardless of how harmless it seems.

Jesus said that it's not what goes into the mouth that makes a man unclean, but what comes out of it. When dealing with guarding the heart, I believe it's imperative to control what goes into the mouth also. There are a number of substances that we ingest that are harmful to us. For some people you'll have to guard the 'alcohol and drug' doorway, for others you'll have to guard the 'eating disorder' and 'gluttony' doorways. Whatever your weakness, stand firm in guarding that gate.

The last two gates (south of the beltline) have to do with sex. When God created us I believe that He had specific purposes in mind for every orifice. Any deviation from their intended use will result in harm, either physically or spiritually. And, although God created us as sexual beings, He designed sex to be enjoyed within the confines of a marriage (between one man and one woman). Sex outside of marriage is sin and is never approved of by God. Having homosexual relations is listed as sin, right between offering children as sacrifices and having sex with animals (see Leviticus 18:21–23). It doesn't matter if you entered homosexuality through choice, abuse or generational curses; it's still sin. God wants to free us from our sin. He wants us to walk in the peace and joy that Jesus died to give us. God created us for more than flesh; He wants to satisfy our spirit.

Guarding the gates is an ongoing task. Anyone who tells you that freedom is free is either still deceived or has never been bound. Freedom costs; a lot. The day that I got saved I told Jesus that if He would lead me, I would follow Him anywhere. Had I known the road that lay ahead, I might not have been so bold.

Friends/Support

It was imperative for me to find people that supported my new lifestyle. The devil will do all he can to draw you back into the pit. Ask God to send you people to stand on the wall with you and for you (see Nehemiah 4:16–18). Resist opening yourself up for ridicule and rejection; allow God to choose your friends. God knows what we need and who can provide it. Stand guard against familiar spirits, even in the church. Jesus warned us that there are wolves in sheep's clothing, and He was talking about people in the church. If you feel immediately drawn to a certain person, ask God to show you if it's a divine connection or a spirit from your past. God will sanctify friendships for us, but He must be the foundation.

It was also imperative for me that connections to my old life were severed. This needed to happen in both the physical and the spiritual realms. Physically, it meant that I eliminated contact with old friends, partners and all acquaintances from my old lifestyle. I got rid of everything associated with my former life, from old birthday cards to clothing from ex-lovers. I had to walk away from absolutely everything, but God has honored my obedience. For people serious about freedom, no price is too great.

Soul Ties

Spiritual separation involves breaking soul ties. Soul ties are exactly what they sound like, a tie between two or more souls. These ties keep us bound and must be broken if we are to be free. I told you that when Pastor Jim prayed for Beth, I manifested. That's because Beth and I had a soul tie. When you have a soul tie with somebody, your spirit is open to theirs, allowing spiritual 'traffic' to go back and forth. I did not have a problem with depression before I met Beth, but she did. By the end of our relationship I was taking medication daily to handle 'my' depression. Throughout our relationship one of us was continually sick or injured. Because of the soul tie we had, the spirit of infirmity traveled freely back and forth between us. The spirits of rage and lust within me transferred to Beth, and in the end we both had more problems than we started with.

Unholy soul ties allow legal access for the devil and his demons. These soul ties are most commonly formed through sexual contact and generational curses (sometimes called bloodline curses). When counseling with people, I often tell them that celibacy protects them from STD's (sexually transmitted demons). In the same way that communicable diseases can be transferred through physical contact, spiritual 'diseases' (like spirits of rage, perversion, addiction, etc.) can be transferred through sexual contact.

A full explanation about soul ties is beyond the scope of this book, but I do want to equip you to identify and break the soul ties in your life. There are some very good books that explain soul ties and legal access. For more information about these topics please see the suggested reading list at the end of this book.

Basically, anyone you have had sex with either physically or emotionally (since God judges the heart, not the action) you have formed a soul tie with. People often wonder why they can never let go of their first love. It is usually because a soul tie was formed. Imagine tying a rope around your waist, with the other end tied to a horse. Everywhere you go the horse has to go too. Conversely, everywhere the horse goes, you have to go. Now, some people just learn to adapt and decide to ride the horse everywhere they go. That may seem fine, but it's somewhat limiting. Let's say you ride your horse to work and get a corner office on the first floor with a window. That allows your horse to stand outside your window and wait for you to finish work. Then you climb through your window, get on your horse and ride home. So far so good. But what happens when you get a promotion and they want to move you to the penthouse office? Now you have to decide whether to take the promotion (and hope your office and the elevator is big enough for your horse) or to stay in your first-floor cubicle. This sounds ridiculous, but it's what we do. We try to move on with our lives, but we're tied down to so many 'horses' that we can't make any progress. Jesus came to heal the broken-hearted and to set the captives free (Isaiah 61:1). You can be free, from all of your horses.

Soul ties are broken through prayer. The Bible promises that God is faithful to complete the good work He has begun in us. In order to break the soul ties we need only to ask God, in Jesus' name, to free us from this spiritual baggage. There is a prayer in Chapter Eleven to assist you in this.

Anger

Anger was not only an emotion in my life, it had become part of my identity. I had used anger to control people, to get my own way and as an excuse for my fits of carnality and self-destructive habits. Anger was much like a drug, allowing otherwise unacceptable behavior to surface. While there was sometimes remorse connected to my anger, it was never enough to make me surrender it.

I told you the story about the day in the locker room that I chose anger. I decided, that day, that I would no longer be on the losing side of rage. By making that choice, I gave the devil legal access to my soul. I thought that anger (and the violence that soon followed) would bring me power. I had seen the 'benefits' of rage in my childhood through Dad: fear, manipulation, submission and control. What I didn't understand was the price that came with befriending anger. I thought that anger would be a tool I could use to make things happen. As it turned out, I became a tool that the devil used to make things happen. I didn't get to choose when I would be angry, it would just come over me like a shadow. Since I was already predisposed to anger through generational curses, I was an easy target for Satan.

Another part of the price in choosing anger was the confusion it created in my mind. I was in a constant battle to keep my body from reacting to the impulses that were planted in my mind. I was continually plotting and planning revenge against whatever perceived injustice I felt I had suffered. The noise in my head was deafening. I have often described it as sounding like a radio between stations; fragments of conversation, snippets of music and ongoing static that makes it almost impossible to concentrate. The noise in my head was so bad that I literally didn't know left from right.

I had been saved for several years before God started dealing with me about my anger. Like so many other areas, I had no idea of where to begin. I read books, studied the Word, and told God I was willing to be willing to let go of my anger. As always, God met me where I was at.

Since anger and I had been so close for so many years, it felt a lot like a break up. Anger had been my friend, and then my lover throughout much of my life. I decided that I would sever our relationship with a 'Dear John' letter. This is an excerpt from my journal:

Dear Anger,
This is a difficult letter to write. I know we've been friends for a long time; more than friends really, probably lovers. You have been there for me when nobody else was. When I was alone and scared you showed up and rescued me. You beat back the villains and built a wall of protection for me. When I didn't know what to think or say, you showed up, protecting me from everybody, myself included.

I remember the day we met, or more appropriately, the day I joined your side. I had known you my whole life, but I never knew you could work for me. I knew the other side of you; the sharp, cutting side that demolished people with a word or a swing, but I didn't know the soft, fuzzy side of you that I felt when you were with me instead of against me. You're like a sword; when Dad had you I always got cut because he had the handle and I got the blade. But, when I figured out how to get the handle, you became my best friend. We went everywhere together; sports, school, jobs, home, relationships, everywhere. You became the only constant; the only thing I knew would always be there.

My life changed that day in the locker room at the rink. Rodney (that broomball coach that was creepy and arrogant all at once) was so surprised when he yelled at me in front of the team and I didn't cry. (Uhgh, before I met you I cried all the time. That was horrible; just a pathetic little girl who was always scared and hurt. Pathetic.) He yelled at me that day because I told him I couldn't play in a game because I had hockey at the same time. He told me I had to make a choice; either be in or out. I almost cried, but then you showed up. I felt your power as I took hold of the handle of the sword. It felt like you made me ten feet tall. Instead of crying I took off my jersey, threw it across the room at him and told him I had made my choice. He could keep his jersey, I was playing hockey. Everyone was so surprised that I didn't cry when he yelled at me. They told me they were proud of me for not crying. That sealed it. Nobody had ever been proud of me for crying. Anger it was!

Everything changed then. I made a decision, with your help of course, that I wasn't crying anymore. I took the sword by the handle and learned to wield it with power. Nobody could touch us. If I wasn't strong enough to beat them physically I would shred them with my words. My sarcasm became as sharp as you were. Then I found the final ingredient; don't care if I live or die. Once I let go of the fear of death we were unstoppable. I couldn't lose a fight because I didn't care if they killed me. No matter how many times I got knocked down, I just got back up. You taught me not only how to manage physical pain, but how to turn it into fuel. Pain became rage, which sharpened the sword and my words. We were powerful.

You got me through high school. Remember the first day of school when that chick grabbed me and threw me against the locker? I was afraid, but then you showed up. You told me what to say and how to say it. By homeroom I was a hero. I had no idea she was the school bully. I had never met her before so I didn't know that she regularly beat people up for kicks. But not me, thanks to you. The tide turned and she got afraid. I don't know how you pulled it off, but I never did end up fighting her. She walked up and punched me at a football game that time but when she hit me it didn't hurt. You told me not to hit her back, just to look at her. Then you told me what to say and she started crying. You were great. I didn't lift a finger and she ran away scared. I didn't have any more trouble after that. I never had to fight anyone else in high school either. You just took me to the top, had me knock over the kingpin, and then I just had to look tough. Thank you for carrying me through. Without you and drugs I never would have survived school. It was so hard and confusing all the time. I was so scared of everyone. I was afraid that I would have to fight someone and you wouldn't be there to protect me. You were my Superman cape.

After high school you continued to carry me. Through all the crazy relationships and bar fights, I wouldn't have survived without you. I wonder now what people saw when they looked at me. It must have been you, because I was still terrified. I learned the walk and the talk to keep them away, but inside I knew I was nothing without you. You were my identity. I was finally holding the handle of the sword instead of having the tip of it on my throat.

Then I got sober and had to quit fighting. I know that was hard on you. It was hard on me too. But we managed, didn't we? We found new ways to cut people with our words. We took it out on the people we played sports with. We took it out on lovers and sometimes we convinced them that that was what they wanted. That wasn't right though, Anger. I'm finding out that a lot of the stuff 'we' did wasn't right.

When I took you in that day in the locker room, I didn't know there was any other way to live. I thought I could choose Dad's side (handle) or Mom's side (blade). I didn't know that I could have someone else defend me and protect me and save me and love me. You did a lot of things for me Anger, but you never loved me. I'm not saying that you should have; you never told me you would, but that's something that I need. It's not enough to win. I need more than just a victory now; I need love. I need to have someone in my life that lives for peace, and teaches me peace. I

know you don't want to hear this Anger, but the war
is over. The time for life and death battles has ended.
I'm not saying that you are no longer useful, but we
have to correct the balance. There are times when I
need to get angry because the situation rightly calls
for it. But I can no longer have you as a lifestyle. You
cannot continue to be my constant companion. You
can no longer be my lover. I have a new Lover and He
won't tolerate you trying to control me. He wants me
to walk in peace, not in torment. He is helping me to
see that not everything you did for me and to me was
beneficial. Some of the time it was very destructive.
Like the times when there was no one to fight with so
you fought with me. All those times I hurt myself
because I couldn't control you, that wasn't right. That
wasn't even me; that was you. It's my fault because I
let you run my life, but that's stopping now.

Anger, I'm breaking up with you. It's a hard decision
because you're telling me that if I leave you, you'll
send back the fear. But you know what? My new
Lover said He would take care of me. He said He
won't let the fear take over like before. And I believe
Him. I believe He's more than enough for me. I
believe that He is stronger, even than you. I believe
He'll never leave me nor forsake me. You never abandoned me Anger, but you didn't treat me right. You
lied to me all the time, telling me to do things that I
didn't want to do. Then, after I did them and felt
guilty, you told me it was my decision. You coerced
me into so many things. You told me that if I took
hold of you I wouldn't have to be afraid, but then I
was just afraid of you. The fear didn't leave; it just
morphed into something different. It's over, Anger.
You are no longer my god. I renounce you in the

name of Jesus. No longer will my teeth be set on edge by the sour grapes of my forefathers. I thought you were a blessing, coming to save me from Dad, but you were just another curse, coming through Dad. I draw the Bloodline. You are finished, Anger. I bind you and I cast you back to the gates of Hell in Jesus' name. You are officially a trespasser in my life. You no longer have legal access to my thoughts, my words, my actions or my decisions. You are a feeling, like joy and sadness and excitement. You will come and then you will go, in Jesus' name. You are no longer my lover, my confidant, my protector or my friend. You have been relegated back to your intended place as a feeling. I'm not saying that you or any other feeling is wrong or bad. I am saying that you will no longer run my life. God is running my life. Jesus has become my Savior. I no longer require you.

I can feel you trying to rise up, trying to make me angry at you. I'm not angry with you. I'm grateful for seeing the truth. The truth is, I may not have survived until now without you. I am grateful for your assistance, but now I'm moving on. Good-bye, Anger.

Sincerely,

Donna

P.S.

If you have any questions, please take it up with God. Thank you.

Some pretty amazing things happened for me after writing this letter. For the first time in my life the noise in my head stopped. I noticed its absence immediately. I was sitting in my apartment and I heard my refrigerator running. I had never heard that before, as the noise had always drowned it out. I called my mentor to tell her about this newfound silence. (I didn't know that not everybody lived with the noise, so I was surprised when I had to explain it to her.) After trying to explain the silence, she told me that it sounded like peace. I couldn't believe it…I had peace!

Another breakthrough came when I realized that I now knew left from right. For thirty years I had struggled with directions and instructions, and now it was so easy. I don't know which was more exciting for me, the peace I had or not feeling like a moron all the time.

Anger still tries to revisit on a fairly consistent basis. It still makes promises that entice my flesh, but the price is more than I'm willing to pay. Peace has become too valuable to me. Anger has become like all my other exes; occasionally it crosses my mind but I thank God that I'm free from it.

Shame

After I was freed from anger, it seemed that shame hit me like a ton of bricks. It affected every area of my life and I felt like I was being crippled by my self-loathing. This is an excerpt from my journal during that struggle.

Shame is like platelets, its just part of my blood. It runs through my body and mind on a continual basis. I am ashamed of who I am, what I am, where I came from and where I'm going. I am ashamed of how I look, how I talk, what I say and how I think. I am ashamed of my body, my weight, my intelligence, my creativity, my talents and my humor. I am ashamed of everything about me. I am ashamed that I am me. I am ashamed that I am.

My arrogance is based in shame—I know I'm not worthy so I try extra hard to make you think I am. I blame other people for everything to protect myself. I already know it's my fault; whatever 'it' is. I am ashamed that I am alive. Mom's first pregnancy miscarried. I am ashamed that he died and I lived. I don't think anyone knows the baby's gender, but I know it was a boy. He should have lived. He may have been able to stop Dad. I couldn't, and I'm ashamed of that too.

There is something fundamentally wrong with being me. Aside from the fact that I don't deserve to live, there's something even more wrong; something disgusting and contagious.

I've never been 'acceptable'. I can't say s's. I'm not built like a girl. If I were a boy it would be acceptable for me to be barrel-chested and have shoulders like a fullback. But I'm not. I tried, hard. I shaved my hair and wore men's clothes and lots of people thought I was a guy. Every time they called me 'sir' it confirmed the fact that I was a mistake. Brenda asked Mom one time if she would ever have a brother. Mom told her that she had me, and that I was as close to a brother as she could get.

I finished reading the codependency book this morning[1]. I knew when I read the shame chapter a couple weeks ago that I would have to come back to it. I reread it this morning. It says (page 106) "Shame can make us feel crazy and do crazy things. It hurts to

believe it's not okay to be who we are. To protect ourselves from that pain, we may avoid shame by turning
it into other feelings that are safer and easier to handle: rage; indifference; an overwhelming need to control; depression; confusion; flightiness; or an
obsession to use our drug of choice, whether that
"drug" is alcohol, a pill, food, sex, or money. We may
transform shame into blame, numbness or panic. Or
we may deal with it by running away." I can look at
my life and watch shame morph from one thing to the
next.

I've always had lots of ways to punish myself for
being alive; drugs, bad relationships, anger, self-
hatred. But now it feels like, since God has set me
free from some of that, the cycle is becoming more
vicious. I loathe myself and my body. I imagine taking a sharp knife and carving myself into the person I
think I should be; not even the person, just the body.
When I think about trying to lose weight I don't think
about cutting back, I think about not eating for 2 or 3
months. I could be religious and call it a fast, but
what it really is is a hunger strike against myself.
Maybe that's what all my fasting is. I don't know.

An ironic twist is that I never felt ashamed of being a
drug addict or an alcoholic. It's like that's what was
expected of me. I was proud of the fact that I could
drink all night and work the next day; that I could do
enough drugs to kill a horse and still drive home. I
was proud of the fact that I could fight. It's like all
that I could do was replicate what Dad did. I hated
him so much, and then I became him.

So what happens now? The root of the shame, I think, is that when I was a baby I was violated in ways too horrible for words. Something inside of me broke, or at least suffered heavy damages. That thing inside of us that tells us that we're okay was stolen, and replaced with a lie that says I'm not okay, that I'm not enough. Now I know whom the thief was. I thought for long time it was Dad, but Dad was only a tool that Satan was using. A long time ago Satan stole that part inside of Dad that said he was okay. So Dad, under the influence of Satan, alcohol and generational curses, followed Satan's directions and hurt me. Satan is a liar and a thief and I hate him. I hate him for hurting me and destroying my family. I hate him for stealing my childhood and my joy. I hate him for trying to still control me through shame and guilt and manipulation. I hate him because he disrespects my God. I hate him because he lies to me and tries to make me not trust people. I hate him because he tells me to throw myself down, with depression, food and self-hatred. I hate him because, up until now, he's been successful. Well guess what, Satan…you lose!

In the all-powerful name of Jesus I bind that spirit of shame. I command you back to gates of hell in Jesus' name. I plead the Blood of Jesus over my thoughts, my memories, my body and myself. I plead the Blood of Jesus over my family. I choose to forgive and bless my Dad for EVERYTHING that has happened. I choose to forgive and bless my Mom for everything she did and everything she failed to do. I choose to forgive and bless Brenda, for all that she was and all that she wasn't. I pray for blessings over every member of my family. I draw the Bloodline in my family and I say NO MORE, Satan. In the name of Jesus I command you to get off of me, get off my family and go back to hell! I will not be directed by shame. I will not be directed by guilt. I will not throw myself down. IT IS WRITTEN at the name of Jesus every knee will bow and every tongue confess that Jesus Christ is Lord. IT IS WRITTEN that He who has begun a good work in me will complete it. IT IS WRITTEN that the effective, fervent prayer of a righteous man avails much. IT IS WRITTEN that I am the head and not the tail. IT IS WRITTEN that the Lord is my strength and my shield; my heart trusts in Him and I am helped. IT IS WRITTEN that I can do everything through Him who gives me strength. IT IS WRITTEN that no weapon formed against me will prosper. I forgive myself, Satan. God forgives me. My family forgives me. I FORGIVE MYSELF. I WILL NOT BE ASHAMED FOR WHO I AM. I WILL NOT BE ASHAMED. AND…I WILL LIVE AND NOT DIE. I CHOOSE LIFE, SATAN, SO GO BACK TO HELL IN JESUS' NAME.

Now, every other spirit that travels with shame, I bind you in Jesus' name and I cast you back to the gates of hell. I bind dread, fear, hate, rage, blame, ego, mania, gluttony, addiction, excess, greed, sloth, envy, jealousy, malice, one-up-man-ship, false confidence, pride, haughtiness, lust, codependence and unhealthy need. I bind you all in Jesus' name and I cast you back to the gates of hell. It is written that that which we bind on earth shall be bound in heaven and that which we loose on earth shall be loosed in heaven. In the name of Jesus I loose peace (that peace which passes all understanding), contentment, self-control, a God-yielding spirit, trust, love, patience, joy unspeakable, hope, humility, prosperity, acceptance, forgiveness and a good future. I release myself from shame and guilt, knowing that God has already released me. I release my family and everyone from my past that has hurt me. Father God, I ask You to release them too. Please do not hold their sin against them. Please give them the same freedom and new life that You have given me. Thank You Father. I love You Lord. All glory to You. In Jesus' name I pray. Amen.

This particular breakthrough came through much prayer and fasting. I had done several Word studies and spent a lot of time reading scriptures. I lived alone at the time, had scriptures taped to every wall of my apartment and played praise and worship music continually. Satan had held me captive with shame for a very long time, and he didn't want to give up now. Thankfully, greater is He who is in us that he that is in the world (1 John 4:4).

Forgiveness

Nobody wants to forgive; at least not initially. It goes against everything in our flesh that cries out for retribution. Forgiveness means that we don't get to hate any more, and that we can no longer blame our entire existence on the mistakes of another.

I didn't want to forgive people because I thought it meant that they got off the hook. I didn't want them off the hook. I wanted them to live like I had lived. I wanted them to suffer, as I felt I had suffered. What I didn't understand was that the same hook that held them in place also had its barbs in me. The hate that fueled my unforgiveness was the anchor that was keeping me stuck.

The Bible says that if we forgive others for their sins then God will forgive us for our sins. It goes on to say that if we don't forgive others then He won't forgive us (Matthew 6:15).

I need God's forgiveness. Every day I make mistakes and every day I fall short of who I know I'm supposed to be. I can't afford not to have God's forgiveness, so I can't afford not to forgive others. Somehow we convince ourselves that there are different levels of sin; that adultery is worse than gossip or that murder is worse than judgment. The Bible says that the wages of sin is death (Romans 6:23). That means, in God's eyes, there is no difference in what Dad did to me, and me judging him for it. Both are sin, and both will lead to death.

Forgiveness is a choice. It is not a feeling or an idea, and it is not something we are able to come to on our own. We make the choice to be willing to forgive and then we let God do the rest. My mentor once told me that the difference between bitterness and joy is our capacity to forgive. I have come to realize that only God can expand my capacity.

One of the things that I pray is that God will teach me to live a lifestyle of forgiveness. I don't want to waste any more time trapped in bitterness over what happened thirty years ago, nor do I want to waste time now over what happened thirty minutes ago. I have to make the choice to let it go. I guarantee that Satan will do his best to bait you into offense. Once offended, it is only a matter of time before offence becomes resentment, which eventually turns to bitterness. Once again, the difference between bitterness and joy is our capacity to forgive. We get to choose which we will walk in.

This was another area that required much prayer and fasting. I had nursed my unforgiveness for decades. Hatred and judgment had become a way of life for me. My road to healing began with the recognition of my own need for forgiveness. I was a sinner, saved by grace. Without the forgiveness that was offered to me through Jesus Christ, I would be destined to spend eternity in hell. Weighing it out, the resentments just aren't worth it. I make a choice, day by day and sometimes minute by minute, to walk in forgiveness. I try very hard, when people offend me, to immediately forgive them in my heart and ask God to bless them. This takes a great deal of discipline and I often fall short. But I believe that God honors our efforts and will meet us where we're at. All we need is the willingness to be willing to forgive.

Codependency

My bondage in the area of relationships was as damaging as any drug addiction I'd ever faced. Growing up in a family with role-reversals, violence and abandonment, I was a perfect candidate for dysfunctional relationships. I grabbed onto whomever I got close to and I wouldn't let go until we were both scarred and bloody. It has been my experience that codependents don't have relationships; they take hostages.

I believe that the basis of codependency is a poor foundation. Without loving parents to nurture and guide you, it is difficult to successfully navigate life. Without healthy, Godly role models, children are forced to develop their own ideas of what relationships are supposed to look like. Unfortunately, children are limited in their thinking by what they have previously been exposed to. Children do not grow up and choose spouses exactly like their parents because they want the pain to continue; they do it because that's the only way they know.

My freedom from codependency came through finding out who I am in Christ. I had to start looking at myself as God saw me, not through the eyes of man. I had to make the choice to believe what was written about me in His Word, instead of what I had heard throughout my life. I was able to find my place in this world only after I found my place in Him. Once my relationship with God was stable, the rest of my relationships started falling into place.

I would encourage anyone struggling with codependency issues to read the book "Love is a Choice". It was an absolute Godsend in helping me sort through the spider-web of rejection, abandonment and identity issues. It provided an explanation for my atrocious behavior in relationships and provided some much-needed sanity for my fractured thinking.

This chapter is by no means a complete list of the issues I've walked through on the road to healing. My hope is that it will provide you with some tools to help you on your walk, and to encourage you that all things are possible through Christ. Remember: God is no respecter of person; what He'll do for one, He'll do for another.

Chapter Ten

*Perseverance must finish its work so that you may be
mature and complete, not lacking anything. If any of
you lacks wisdom, he should ask God, who gives
generously to all without finding fault.*

James 1:4–5

There are a lot of tough questions that are raised by people dealing with homosexuality. I had a lot of questions but no one to ask. My friends were as deceived as I was, I had already convinced my family to accept my lifestyle, and I was receiving bad advice from the church. I truly didn't know who I could trust to tell me the truth. The only reason I kept looking for answers was because I felt God leading me. I am so grateful that He never gives up on us.

In this chapter I'm going to try to answer some of the questions that I battled with. My hope is that this will help you find resolution also.

Is being gay wrong?

According to God it is. Leviticus 18:22 calls homosexuality a detestable sin, and Leviticus 20:13 goes on to say that the penalty for homosexuality is death.

That's Old Testament stuff; don't we live under the New Testament?

We do live under the new covenant because Jesus gave His life as an atoning sacrifice for our sins. However, even in the New Testament we are told that it is wrong. 1 Corinthians 6:9–10 states, "Do you not know that the unrighteous will not inherit the kingdom of God? Do not be deceived. Neither fornicators, nor idolaters, nor adulterers, nor homosexuals, nor sodomites, nor thieves, nor covetous, nor drunkards, nor revilers, nor extortioners will inherit the kingdom of God."

Does God make people gay?

No, He doesn't. When God created people He made them in His own image (male and female). Immediately after God blessed the man and woman He had created, His first command to them was "be fruitful and increase in number…" (see Genesis 1:27–28). If either the man or the woman had been gay, this plan would not have been unsuccessful.

If I wasn't born gay, then how come I've felt like this my whole life?

In the same way that we can be born with a genetic predisposition for health issues like heart disease, we can also be born with spiritual predispositions. Within the church these are commonly referred to as bloodline curses or generational curses.

I was predisposed to many things, both physically and spiritually. My height and the color of my eyes were determined by my bloodline, as were my rage and sexual preference. In Exodus 20 we are told that the sins of the father will be visited upon the children to the third and forth generations of those who hate God. Thankfully, we are also told that God will show His love to a thousand generations of those who love Him and keep His commands.

As I stated earlier, I sometimes tell people I was raised by orangutans. I was born into a viper's nest of addiction, perversion and hate. My ancestors did not love God or follow His commands, so I was born into their curses. Fortunately for all of us, these curses can be broken. When Jesus died on the cross He bore all of my sin and shame. Jesus died, in my place, so that the curses in my life could be broken. The Blood of Jesus is more powerful than any bloodline curse. All we need to do is to ask for forgiveness, repent of our sins and ask God to break those curses in Jesus' name. There is a prayer in the following chapter to help you in this area.

I don't think any of my ancestors were gay. Why am I?

The spirit of perversion can be displayed in various forms. It may manifest as homosexuality, sexual abuse, fornication, adultery, etc. When considering whether or not you may be under a bloodline curse, look for these behaviors or similar patterns. The other thing to keep in mind is that, even two generations ago, homosexuality was still a well-kept secret. It would be unlikely that the family would broadcast it if great-aunt Fannie were a lesbian.

If being gay is wrong why do I have these feelings?

The flesh is really only interested in things that make it feel good. Feelings operate closely with the flesh. Humans are often described as triune beings; composed of body, mind and spirit. The body basically wants satisfaction; usually attained through food and sex. The spirit wants relationship with God. The mind (thoughts and emotions) is pulled back and forth between body and spirit. 2 Corinthians 10:5 gives us instruction on how to handle this battle, "We demolish arguments and every pretension that sets itself up against the knowledge of God, and we take captive every thought to make it obedient to Christ". We get to choose which side we're going to nourish: the flesh or the spirit. Keep in mind, whichever dog you feed is going to grow!

I can't control how I feel. Why does God let this happen?

Feelings can be dangerous because they are so circumstance-dependant. People sometimes get angry and feel like killing someone. The feeling won't put them in jail, but following through with the action will. During the process of walking out your deliverance you may still battle with feelings and attractions. The important thing is to take those thoughts captive and to line up your heart with the Word of God. Thoughts and feelings are like birds flying in the air: it's not your fault if one flies over head, but if you invite it in to build a nest in your hair then you've got problems.

God is compassionate, kind, loving and just. It's not God who makes a woman cheat on her husband, and it's not God that makes a man abuse a child. All evil, including homosexuality, comes from Satan and is designed to create a wall between man and God. Sin separates us from God. Isaiah 59: 1–3 states, "Surely the arm of the Lord is not too short to save, nor his ear too dull to hear. But your iniquities have separated you from God; your sins have hidden his face from you, so that he will not hear". God never turns away from anyone who is seeking Him, but our decisions and actions often turn us away from Him.

If being gay is wrong how come some of the churches allow it?

There are lots of things that go on in the church that God doesn't approve of. God never intended for pastors to fall into adultery, for priests to abuse young boys or for ministries to take advantage of people for financial gain, yet all of these things happen in the church. James 3:1 says that those who teach will be judged more strictly. My heart is deeply grieved for all of those who misrepresent God's truth.

Doesn't God love everybody?

Absolutely. God created each and every one of us for a special purpose and He loves us all as His own children. God loves us so much that He gives us free choice; we get to decide whether or not we love Him back. Jesus said, "If you love me, you will obey what I command" (John 14:15). Lots of people that God loves will end up in hell, but God doesn't send them there. He allows us to choose our own actions, and therefore our eternal destination.

God's love allows Him to forgive our sins completely. However, just because He loves us doesn't mean that we can do whatever we want without consequence. When David committed adultery with Bathsheba, God didn't stop loving him. And when David asked for God's forgiveness it was granted. But the consequence of David's sin remained and as a result David's son died (see 2 Samuel 11–12).

Will God forgive me?

Completely. In John 8:3–11 the Pharisees (religious folk) brought a woman to Jesus who had been caught in adultery. They wanted Him to condemn her for her sin and sentence her to be stoned. Jesus told the people that whomever was without sin should cast the first stone. One by one they walked away until it was only Jesus and the woman left. Jesus did not condemn her, He simply told her "Go now and leave your life of sin".

That's what God wants to do for you. He wants you to receive His forgiveness and leave your life of sin.

Chapter Eleven

Jesus said, "If you hold to my teaching, you are really my disciples. Then you will know the truth, and the truth will set you free."

John 8:31–32

Freedom is not an event, it is a lifestyle. There is freedom from homosexuality. There is freedom from unforgiveness. There is freedom from brokenness. We can walk in love, joy, peace, patience, goodness, gentleness, faithfulness, kindness and self-control. We can have life and have it to the full. We can have all of this because Jesus died for our freedom. Jesus went to the cross, for my sin and for yours. Jesus loves me and He loves you. He's waiting for you to ask Him into your heart. The Bible tells me that I am already clean because of the word Jesus has spoken over me (John 15:3). You can be clean too. Whether you're struggling with porn, perversion, adultery or homosexuality, Jesus can save you. He can fill the emptiness within us. Jesus can heal the brokenness in our lives. You are accepted in the Beloved. Jesus loves you just as you are, but He loves you too much to leave you there.

If you are ready to be free I invite you to pray this prayer aloud:

Jesus, I need your help. I'm a sinner and I don't want to be this way anymore. Help me Jesus. I invite You to come into my life. I ask You to be my Lord. I ask for

*Your forgiveness. I recognize that You are the Son of
God, that You died on the cross for my sins and that
You rose again on the third day. I know that You are
now sitting at the right hand of God, making inter-
cession for me. Come into my life, Lord Jesus. I pray
that You free me from the bondage of my past. I pray
that You heal me from rejection and pain. I pray that
You free me from this lifestyle and teach me to live a
Godly life. I want to change, Lord. Please come into
my heart and come into my thoughts. Come into my
pain and set me free. I love You, Lord. In Jesus' name
I pray. Amen.*

Congratulations. You have just made the most important
decision of your life.

If you have soul ties in your life that need to be broken
pray this prayer aloud as well:

*Lord, I want to be free. In order to be free I am ask-
ing You to cut every ungodly soul tie in my life. I plead
the Blood of Jesus over myself and I pray that You
would cut the spiritual tie between myself and (name
all of the people you have soul ties with). I make a
choice right now God, to forgive them and to forgive
myself. I ask that You bless them and help them to find
freedom in You. I pray cleansing over myself and I ask
that You set me free. I love You, Lord. In Jesus' name I
pray. Amen.*

If you believe you have been born into generational or
bloodline curses then you need to pray against those as well.
These may include behavioral issues (addictions, violence,
perversion, etc.), emotional issues (depression, anxiety,

mental illness, etc.) and/or spiritual issues (witchcraft, occult involvement, etc.). It is wise to seek God's counsel in this, asking Him to reveal to you areas that you may not readily see. Once you have determined the bloodline curses, pray the following prayer:

Lord, I thank You that Your Word says that that which we bind on earth shall be bound in heaven, and that which we loose on earth shall be loosed in heaven. In Jesus' name I bind the bloodline curse of (specifically name each curse that you believe is in your bloodline). I plead the Blood of Jesus over myself, over my family and over my bloodline. No longer will my teeth be set on edge by the sour grapes of my forefathers. I make the choice to forgive my family and to forgive myself. I ask You Lord, in Jesus' name to loose peace, hope and joy in my bloodline. I ask You to forgive my sins, and sins of my forefathers. I thank You, Father. In Jesus' name I pray. Amen.

You have just entered a new beginning. The Bible says, "If we confess our sins, he is faithful and just and will forgive us our sins and purify us from all unrighteousness." (1 John 1:9). You, my friend, have been forgiven and purified. Welcome, to the life that God intended for you. God bless you.

Here are some basic steps to keep you on track:

1. Get a Bible and read it daily. It is imperative that you learn the truth about God, His Word and His character.
2. Pray, without ceasing. Prayer only means talking to God. It doesn't have to be fancy or articulate, just honest. Make every request "in Jesus' name".

That's the stamp that gets your request to God's throne. I have found that fasting is also beneficial during particularly difficult times. If you have a history of eating disorders, consult your pastor before starting a fast.

3. Stop engaging in ungodly behaviors. We submit to God, resist the devil and he must flee. If you are in a homosexual or ungodly relationship, get out of it. Ask God how and He will show you.

4. Get connected to a Bible-based church. This isn't a battle you should try to fight on your own.

5. Guard the gates to your heart (as discussed in Chapter Nine)

6. Talk to someone who understands deliverance and ask him/her to help you.

7. Break the soul ties and generational curses in your life.

8. Ask God for a mentor (a godly person with no ulterior motives) to keep you accountable and meet with them regularly. BE HONEST. If you make a bad decision, make a new decision. Press on.

9. Ask God to choose your friends for you. It is likely that many people will be removed from your life. Do not fear. God is with you.

10. Get rid of everything of the old. This includes photos, mementos, and anything that glorifies perversion. This may include your music and video collections. Don't worry, God will replace it all in due time with items that bless you instead of curse you.

11. It may be beneficial for you to relocate for a time. Be open to God's will and be willing to submit to whatever His plan is for you.

12. Increase time spent on steps 1 and 2.

Chapter Twelve

"You intended to harm me, but God intended it for good to accomplish what is now being done, the saving of many lives."

Genesis 50:20

God is a god of both redemption and restoration. I have told you a lot about my childhood, my family and my past, but I would like to close by telling you about my present.

My dad, the sadistic alcoholic of my childhood, found Jesus in the early '90's and is a born-again believer. He was the first person to buy me a Bible after I got saved and was one of my greatest supporters when I lived as a missionary. He now lives a quiet life with Mary, his second wife. Dad and Mary attend church regularly and are active members in their church and community. He went back to school several years ago to study horticulture. Watching him patiently tend to fragile plants, one would never guess that he was once a dangerous, highly trained killer. He has been sober for many years now and there is no trace of the man that he once was. He has been restored to the peaceful, God-fearing man that he was called to be. All glory to God.

Mom retired from nursing and now spends much of her time with her grandchildren. A few years ago I had the privilege of baptizing her, as she too has dedicated her life to

Christ. She attends church, hosts Bible studies and prays regularly. She is no longer ruled by fear or controlled by codependency. She now lives to please God, not man. We currently live in different countries but we stay in close contact. Our relationship has been restored through the power of God's love. All glory to God.

My sister still reads her Bible, prays daily and continues to seek God's will for her life. Brenda has two beautiful children and she is doing her best to raise them to be men of God. Nicholas, Brenda's youngest, was born with Down Syndrome. He has a variety of physical and cognitive impairments, but we are believing for his complete healing. Jesse, her oldest, is bright and articulate with a sharp sense of humor. Brenda and I now have a great relationship and I consider her to be one of my closest friends.

The salvation of my extended family continues to be a point of prayer for me. A couple of years ago Aunt Anna (the woman who was too drunk to effectively spy on us as children) got saved and is now serving God. She is a Kingdom supporter and is striving daily to become the woman that God has called her to be. Many of my other relatives are still living in chaos and sin, but I believe that God is big enough to pull them out as well.

I am extremely grateful that God has restored my relationship with my biological family. I am also very grateful that He has raised up a spiritual family for me as well. God has brought people into to my life to support me, encourage me, love me and correct me. He has given me Godly examples to follow and mentors to emulate. As I said before, this is not a battle we should fight alone. I thank God for my family, my friends, my mentor and my church.

My life continues to be a work-in-progress, but at least I'm not alone in the battle. I no longer struggle with homosexuality but I have plenty of work left to do in other areas. Someone recently asked me what it felt like to be free from that lifestyle. I didn't really know how to describe it other than to say that I had peace. It's hard to put into words what it feels like when the screaming madness finally stops. It's quiet, and a little unnerving at first. I feel like I fit; not necessarily with all the people around me, but I fit with God. That's a really cool place to be.

It takes a long time to get free from thirty years of junk, but freedom is possible. I know that God did it for me, and I know that He'll do it for you. If you ask Him and if you obey, all things are possible. All glory to God.

Chapter Thirteen

Dealing with Homosexuality in the Church— A Word to Pastors

My goal in writing this book is to not only equip people in their individual struggles, but also to provide some guidance for those to whom these struggling people will look to for help. It has been my experience that most churches are ill prepared to effectively counsel people in this area, and some do more harm than good.

As social and political circles continue to push the 'gay agenda' forward, the church, for the most part, has buried its head in the sand. Sadly, the same mass deception that has swept the nation is finding its way into the church, leading some denominations to allow gays and lesbians to minister from their pulpits. I believe that this practice is playing directly into Satan's hand.

In Chapter Nine I discussed our tendency to classify sin into various categories. The Bible tells us that the wages of sin is death. It doesn't specify which sin; it infers all sin. The Word also tells us that Jesus died for our sins; again, inferring all sin. Jesus died for the homosexual just like He died for the murderer and the gossip. The church however, seems to have an easier time reaching out and forgiving those who have committed sins that are more 'socially acceptable' than homosexuality. I think the basis of this is ignorance; most people simply cannot relate to this particular struggle. Most men can understand a guy dealing with lust, but not lust for another man. The whole idea is repulsive to most people. The challenge that we face as a church is, how do we love the sinner despite the repulsion we feel toward the sin? The answer is to act like Jesus.

A friend of mine is an evangelist who frequently travels to India and Africa for youth conferences. I once heard him say that the smell of someone with leprosy is the most repugnant odor he has ever encountered. He went on to say that he believes that is also the smell of Jesus. Matthew 8:1–4 is an account of one of the miracles performed by Jesus. It states that a man with leprosy knelt before Jesus and said, "Lord, if you are willing, you can make me clean." Jesus reached out His hand, touched the man and said, "I am willing. Be clean." The man was immediately cured of his leprosy.

The challenge that stands before us is this: are we willing to reach out, touch sinners and make them clean? Are we willing to love the unlovable? Are we willing to hug the unhuggable? Are we willing to listen, with an open heart, to those whose sin we can't comprehend? Are we willing to act like Jesus?

I believe that most people who work in ministry do want to be like Jesus. Despite our own quirks and brokenness, we want to display Christ to others and to see souls won for the Kingdom. But often, we need help. This is by no means a complete list, but I would like to offer some tools to use when dealing with someone who is struggling with homosexuality.

Receive Them in Love

One of the most damaging facets of homosexuality is the isolation that most people face. Although some homosexuals are very 'out', the majority of them are living their lives, at least to some extent, in secret. There is a tremendous amount of rejection, often from families, peers and the church. It takes a great deal of courage for someone to come to a pastor or a counselor and ask for help.

It is important when dealing with people struggling with homosexuality to separate the sin from the person. God hates sin, but loves the sinner. We must do likewise. Encourage the person by telling them that there is hope; that they can be delivered from that lifestyle. Also, let them know that you recognize how much courage it took for them to confide in you. Congratulate them on their willingness to seek help. Above all, let them know that they are loved: by you, by the church and by God. Remind them that we are identified by our relationship with Christ, not by our sins.

Before any in-depth discussion about sin or deliverance takes place, be sure to know the status of their salvation. If they have not accepted Jesus as their Lord and Savior then any further work is futile. Again, this is not a battle that should be fought alone. I don't believe this fight can be won without Jesus Christ as our foundation.

Recognize the spectrum of homosexuality

Sexuality, like many issues, covers a broad spectrum. There will be people who come to you who are currently living a homosexual lifestyle, and there will be people who had one experience years ago that has haunted them ever since. One of the ladies I counseled had spent twenty years thinking she was a lesbian because when she was five she and another girl lifted up their skirts. Somehow, through that experience and a myriad of other problems, she was convinced she was gay. An honest discussion revealed that she did not, in her heart, desire relations with women. We prayed for God's forgiveness and cleansing, and she was set free.

Whether the sin has been carried out physically or emotionally, the person will still need to be led through a prayer of repentance. God judges the heart, so He doesn't distinguish between a sexual encounter and a fantasy. Remind the person that God's forgiveness is available for all who ask, and that we are made into new creations in Christ Jesus.

Know what the Bible says about homosexuality

The majority of the people coming to you already know that homosexuality is a sin, but they're going to want to know why. If they've spent any time in a gay-positive church they may know the scriptures better than you do. It's important to be able to give a biblically based answer to their questions, as there may be a great temptation to offer your opinion. Opinions, regardless of how well prepared they are, do not set people free. Leviticus, Romans, 1 Corinthians and 1 Timothy all make reference to this subject, but be careful not to let homosexuality outweigh the love of God in your discussions.

How to respond to a confession of homosexuality

Hopefully, in response to any confession, the person is met with a listening ear, a compassionate heart and a willingness to help. These are the same qualities that are needed here. It is important to let the person know that freedom is available, if that is what they seek. I have found that sugarcoating sin, of any kind, only leads to prolonged deception. It is imperative that people hear the truth about homosexuality and that they hear it in love.

It will likely be beneficial to set up regular sessions with the person for the first few months. The walk out of homosexuality is very lonely and can be utterly confusing. I lost more friends and family when I 'went straight' than I did when I came out as a lesbian. It is imperative that the person has at least one person who continually speaks truth into their situation. If you are unable to fulfill this role yourself, then refer them to a suitable alternative. Keep in mind though that many secular programs may discourage the person from seeking another lifestyle, as society in general has developed an accepting view of homosexuality.

Do I really need to know about all of this?

It is a commonly accepted fact that approximately ten percent of the population is gay. On average, you can count the number of people in your church, divide it by ten, and that will give you an estimation of how many people we're dealing with. That ten percent does not consider the other lives touched by homosexuality, such as parents, siblings, children and spouses. This issue is simply too big to be ignored.

What can I do to help?

- Pray
  - The church needs to reach these souls that are quietly going to hell. Consider asking your intercessory prayer team to start praying that God would bring these lost souls into your church.
  - Therefore confess your sins to each other and pray for each other so that you may be healed. The prayer of a righteous man is powerful and effective (James 5:16)

- For we do not wrestle against flesh and blood, but against principalities, against powers, against the rulers of the darkness of this age, against spiritual hosts of wickedness in the heavenly places (Ephesians 6:12)

- Stay in the Word
  - The more we study God's Word, the easier it is to act like Jesus.
  - For the word of God is living and powerful, and sharper than any two-edged sword, piercing even to the division of soul and spirit, and of joints and marrow, and is a discerner of the thoughts and intents of the heart (Hebrews 4:12)

- Imitate Jesus
  - As we imitate Christ people will be drawn to us. Ask God to prepare your heart for the people He is going to bring into your life and your church.
  - …He has sent me to heal the brokenhearted, to proclaim liberty to the captives, and the opening of the prison to those who are bound (Isaiah 61:1)

- Shepherd the flock
  - Know your congregation and the issues they struggle with. Don't be afraid to give people the truth, even if it's unpopular.
  - Recognize that not everyone is who they seem to be. Provide a safe environment for their issues to surface.

- Keep seeking God
  - Ask, and it will be given to you; seek, and you will find; knock, and it will be opened to you. For everyone who asks receives, and he who seeks finds, and to him who knocks it will be opened (Matthew 7:7–8)

Be Encouraged

2 Timothy 3:16 says, "All Scripture is given by inspiration of God, and is profitable for doctrine, for reproof, for correction, and for instruction in righteousness, that the man of God may be complete, thoroughly equipped for every good work." God has equipped you thoroughly for every good work…including this one.

It is God's will that not one will be lost. I appreciate your taking time to read this book. It is my hope that, through this work, souls will be saved and hearts will be set free. Thank you again. All glory to God!

Suggested Reading List

The Bible
 (my preferred translations are New International Version
 (NIV) and New King James Version (NKJV) but all are
 good. Find one that speaks to you.)

Battlefield of the Mind
 by Joyce Meyer

Shadow Boxing: The Dynamic 2-5-14 Strategy to
 Defeat the Darkness Within
 by Henry Malone

Breaking Unhealthy Soul Ties
 by Bill Banks and Sue Banks

Love is a Choice—Breaking the Cycle of Addictive
 Relationships
 by Robert Hemfelt, Frank Minirth and Paul Meier

Codependent No More: How to Stop Controlling Others and
 Start Caring for Yourself
 by Melody Beattie

Beyond Codependency: And Getting Better All the Time
 by Melody Beattie

The Bait of Satan
 by John Bevere

Daddy Loves His Girls
  by T.D. Jakes

The Father Heart of God
  by Floyd McClung, Jr.

A Tale of Three Kings
  by Gene Edwards

Spiritual Authority
  by Watchman Nee

---

[1] Beyond Codependency by Melody Beattie

Printed in the United States
82653LV00001B/13-78/A